The Hammock

MARLENA COMPSTON

LifeRich
PUBLISHING®

LifeRich Publishing is a registered trademark of The Reader's Digest Association, Inc.

LifeRich Publishing books may be ordered through booksellers or by contacting:

LifeRich Publishing
1663 Liberty Drive
Bloomington, IN 47403
www.liferichpublishing.com
844-686-9607

Because of the dynamic nature of the Internet, any web addresses or links contained in this book may have changed since publication and may no longer be valid. The views expressed in this work are solely those of the author and do not necessarily reflect the views of the publisher, and the publisher hereby disclaims any responsibility for them.

Holy Bible, New International Version®, NIV® Copyright ©1973, 1978, 1984, 2011 by Biblica, Inc.® Used by permission. All rights reserved worldwide.

Any people depicted in stock imagery provided by Getty Images are models, and such images are being used for illustrative purposes only. Certain stock imagery © Getty Images.

ISBN: 978-1-4897-4488-3 (sc)
ISBN: 978-1-4897-4487-6 (hc)
ISBN: 978-1-4897-4492-0 (e)

Library of Congress Control Number: 2022919713

Print information available on the last page.

LifeRich Publishing rev. date: 12/08/2022

To My Children
Alicia, Ross, Keith

Introduction

THE HAMMOCK was written to extend a beautiful opportunity for you to seek and pursue a dwelling place for your heart. It is my desire to share my own quiet moments, peaceful times, and places that my heart has chosen to dwell. In this busy world we share, I have found it necessary to seek out and steal away precious moments of solitude for my spirit to not only unwind but to seek out that still and small whisper calling me to fellowship with my Heavenly Father.

SOME of my very favorite moments are those spent in my hammock. Moments spent sitting at the very foot of the Cross with my heart completely surrendered to Him. A soft pillow for my head and wrapped up in my favorite blanket, the Holy Spirit begins to usher in peace as the hammock gently rocks me.... a most definite oasis for my heart. The hammock has allowed me the freedom to have moments alone, to bask in His joy and, at times, to stain my pillow with tears. Many prayers have been prayed in my hammock. Prayers prayed for my children. Prayers for direction, wisdom, and healing. Salvation and deliverance for family members. Cries to a Holy Father from, sometimes, a prodigal daughter. Times of oppression or sorrow that my Father would remind me in these moments that though I'm weak...He is strong. Many a morning the Lord God and I have spent with the birds chirping and the sun rising. We've shared many an evening together under a full blanket of stars. This place.... my hammock... has proven many times to be holy ground. Find, today, that place that brings you the very closest to our Heavenly Father. He's waiting for you.

Marlena ♥

Glimpse of Glory

He leads me beside still waters; He restores my soul.
Psalm 23:2-3

ZAC DURANT

Somedays are just not glorious. The sun shines brightly but we still get burned. The moon sets itself beautifully in the night sky to find us awake and not sleeping. Life can have moments... even days...of unrest. With unrest and turmoil comes a time that you finally yield and give it all up. It's always amazing to me that in our human flesh we struggle to 'find the answer' to whatever the 'issue' is. We must maneuver through some relationships trying to not step on explosive mines. We put our heart 'out there' only to have it shoved right back at us. Sometimes letting out a few misplaced words seems to feel better than lifting our hands in praise when we're discouraged or feel let down.

As I opened the Word tonight, Psalm 23 came to mind. Turning pages, there it was. Just ten small words ready to breathe peace into my soul. The words are very clear...He, my Heavenly Father who loves me, tenderly leads, and guides me beside still and peaceful waters. He, the Lord who created me restores, strengthens, and holds my soul. No need to be troubled.

No need to doubt. No need to be discouraged or want to shut down after you feel let down. Just a time to sit back and gather peace. Feel the cool fan blow on my warm face and know, without a doubt, that tomorrow is a new day.

Thank You, Father God, for a little glimpse of Your glory.

♥ Write out Psalms 23 in your own words.

_____

_____

_____

_____

_____

_____

_____

_____

_____

_____

_____

_____

Breathe in Love

And this is my prayer: that your love may abound
more and more in knowledge and depth of insight, so
that you may be able to discern what is best and may
be pure and blameless until the day of Christ, filled
with the fruit of righteousness that comes through
Jesus Christ—to the glory and praise of God.
Philippians 1:9-11

EUGENE ZHYVCHIK

What if we chose today to breathe in love and breathe out
anything within us that keeps us from kingdom living...here
on earth. Things like bitterness, unforgiveness, hurt, worry,
depression, fear, jealousy....to name a few. And to think if we
will make a choice to expel those from our souls, then they
would melt off us and no longer have any power over us to zap
our strength or steal our joy. It is such an easier path to walk

when we choose to love and NOT accept the invitation to get on the merry-go-round ride of emotions that can control every single moment of every single day.... if we allow.

May we be encouraged today and know that we have the power within us, through Christ, to breathe in love. May our love abound more and more each day.

What A Man

What a man Jesus has always proven to be.

As a baby, Jesus caught the attention of the whole world. As a young teen, He could be found teaching in the synagogue already showing wisdom beyond His years. As He walked on this Earth, fulfilling the call on His life, He showed great qualities of what a man should be. He was first a **SERVANT**... Matthew 29:28 "just as the Son of Man did not come to be served, but to serve, and to give His life a ransom for many." Ever **LOYAL** to His followers and always had their best at heart. He **VALUED CHILDREN** and showed them they were not only valuable but also greatly loved – He was not afraid or 'too manly' to show affection...Mark 10:16 "And He took them up in His arms, laid His hands on them, and blessed them." He allowed Himself to be placed under authority and **FOLLOWED** that **AUTHORITY** to the very end.... John 5:29 "Then Jesus answered and said to them 'Most assuredly, I say to you, the Son can do nothing of Himself, but what He sees the Father do; for whatever He does the Son also does in like manner.' He was a **GREAT LISTENER** and **FRIEND**. He was a **COMPASSIONATE** man that felt the sorrows of those around Him. One of my favorite qualities about Jesus is He was (and still is!) **REAL.** He didn't put up with, what I call, the spirit of religiosity. He called a spade a spade. He didn't choose to hang with the proud Pharisees because He knew they had no intention of swallowing their pride and opening their hearts. Instead, He chose to **SPEND TIME** with those that truly mattered and those that wanted a change in their life. A repentant heart He could not deny or turn away from. Psalm 51:17 "The sacrifice acceptable to God is a broken spirit; a broken and contrite heart, O God, thou wilt not despise." Lastly, He is and will always be a beautiful picture of the perfect **LOVER** as He extended His arms and breathed His last breath...for you and for me. Refer to the Cross. What a man. What a Savior.

♥ Describe your relationship with Jesus. Do you feel close to Him, or does He seem far away? Ask Him to reveal Himself to you through His Word.

_____

_____

_____

_____

_____

_____

_____

_____

_____

_____

_____

_____

Today is Your Day of Salvation

Amazing words. ♥ So much wisdom and truth. Wrap your head and heart around each one. Meditate on them. Allow the Holy Spirit to teach you. If you have not taken that step quite yet, TODAY can be YOUR day of salvation. ♦

"You, my brothers and sisters, were called to be free. But do not use your freedom to indulge the flesh; rather, serve one another humbly in love. For the entire law is fulfilled in keeping this one command: "Love your neighbor as yourself." If you bite and devour each other, watch out or you will be destroyed by each other. So I say, walk by the Spirit, and you will not gratify the desires of the flesh. For the flesh desires what is contrary to the Spirit, and the Spirit what is contrary to the flesh. They conflict with each other, so that you are not to do whatever you want. But if you are led by the Spirit, you are not under the law. The acts of the flesh are obvious: sexual immorality, impurity, and debauchery; idolatry and witchcraft; hatred, discord, jealousy, fits of rage, selfish ambition, dissensions, factions, and envy; drunkenness, orgies, and the like. I warn you, as I did before, that those who live like this will not inherit the kingdom of God. But the fruit of the Spirit is love, joy, peace, forbearance, kindness, goodness, faithfulness, gentleness, and self-control. Against such things there is no law. Those who belong to Christ Jesus have crucified the flesh with its passions and desires. Since we live by the Spirit, let us keep in step with the Spirit. Let us not become conceited, provoking, and envying each other." Galatians 5:13-26

♥ Are you saved? Do you have total assurance of your salvation? If not, let's take care of that today. Write your prayer below in your own words, or the following: "Father God, I confess I am a sinner and in need of a Savior. Thank You for cleansing me of all my sin as I accept Jesus Christ as my Lord and Savior. Heal my heart, Lord, and fill me with Your Spirit. Amen."

_____

_____

_____

_____

_____

_____

_____

_____

BEN WHITE

My Heart is His

Delight yourself in the Lord, and He will
give you the desires of your heart,
Psalm 37:4

Life happens.

It's so easy to allow so many things to pull us. My heart can be tugged to the left and to the right. Something I can always count on....my heart is His. As I meditate on the story of the woman at the well and read a commentary, it's so interesting to know that Jesus met her right where she was at. She didn't have to "clean up" for Him. He offered her living water...He offered Himself. One commentary said "The woman at the well had her sins 'washed away' by Jesus. The story shows that Jesus offers divine mercy in the living water of grace, which washes away sins and cleanses souls. The woman went to the well, in the heat of the day, to get a jug of water. Instead, she got much more, including a cleansed and refreshed spiritual life." She had looked for her life companion and, in fact, met Him that day at the well. She came to the realization that nothing...and certainly no one...could fill her besides Him. Life companion indeed...He would never leave her. He would always provide for her. He would always understand her. Living water in her dry, parched world.

My heart is His. He has never misled me. His word is truth... if He said it, I can then assuredly bank on it being so. He has a great plan and, this woman, loves knowing there is a PLAN. As I learn, more and more, to completely surrender to Him, He continues to take my hand and steal my heart. Amazing that the distractions do continue to come my way but it's my desire and responsibility to keep myself looking forward and to continue to seek His face. It's when I look behind me, at the distraction, that I'm pulled away from the Force that sustains me. Sometimes life is about adjusting and re-adjusting and choosing obedience and continuing to fall in love with the One who knows me fully.

My heart is His. That's just the way it is. I never doubt or question this fact. I wake up knowing I 'belong". I go to sleep knowing I STILL BELONG. For anyone that has experienced rejection, loss, upheaval, devastation, or asked questions of where they fit in this world...He offers life companionship to you as well. Choose life, the WORD says, choose Him.

♥ How did this devotion stir your heart? Write your own love letter below.

_____

_____

_____

_____

_____

_____

_____

_____

_____

_____

Choose Obedience

Have I not commanded you? Be strong and courageous.
Do not be afraid; do not be discouraged, for the Lord
your God will be with you wherever you go.
Joshua 1:9 NIV

JAMETLENE RESKP

Joshua was preparing the people of Israel to cross the Jordan River. Little did they know the miracles that were in the very near future. Read this chapter and notice that their hearts were ready. They were prepared to do whatever was asked of them. Obedience. Willing obedience. They wanted better for their nation, their families, and for themselves. Moses had passed away. God had placed Joshua in charge, and he took this responsibility very seriously.

Place yourself in their shoes…if they even had shoes to wear. They weren't any different than we are today. Certainly, the times were different, but they needed a home to protect them from the elements, and food for nourishment, as well as clothing. They needed God, and for Him to deliver them safely to their new land.

Lord, help us to choose obedience every time. Not grumble. Not choose to rebel. Not question. I know You will show Yourself faithful, as You always do. Amen.

♥ Hebrews 4:12 states, "For the word of God is alive and active. Sharper than any double-edged sword, it penetrates even to dividing soul and spirit, joints, and marrow; it judges the thoughts and attitudes of the heart." Are you living in disobedience? Rebellion? Let's repent and take care of those things today.

_____

_____

_____

_____

_____

_____

_____

_____

_____

_____

_____

_____

Trust His Timing

Trust in the LORD with all your heart and
lean not on your own understanding.
Proverbs 3:5

There is a time when it seems that nothing is working out the way you had hoped. You felt the Lord give you a direction and then...you reason you might have heard Him wrong. Could it be that it simply isn't His time?

For days now my heart keeps going back to Esther. Esther was in exactly the place she was supposed to be at precisely the right time, <u>but</u> she had to wait to know when it was time to go before the King. She heeded the words of her uncle, she waited patiently, and she was shown great favor when her time had finally come to approach the throne. As the story goes, she had great favor with the king, and was instrumental in the deliverance of her people.

What have you been waiting for? Does it feel like your dreams will never be realized? THIS BOOK is a perfect example in my own life of...waiting. I KNEW over a dozen years ago it would happen! I am continually praying 'God...I love You. I thank You for my life and every blessing." Today, I am praying "God, HELP ME to trust You more...to lean on You more... to better understand Your ways and Your perfect TIME. Lord, You know I can get impatient and get in my own way. Place me on that 'cliff of trust' that I must fall backwards into Your arms and know...and that You are going to catch me. You have a plan, a purpose, the perfect provision for me. I am CHOOSING to trust that plan, purpose and provision to come to full fruition."

Today I simply place this at Your feet, Lord. That's all that I can do. It's possibly all that You wanted me to do in the first place...to simply TRUST You and trust in Your perfect TIME.

♥ Do you have something you are waiting on? Praying for? Write it below, and place a date on it...day, month, and year.

_____/_____/_____

_____

_____

_____

_____

_____

_____

_____

_____

_____

But do not forget this one thing, dear friends:
With the Lord a day is like a thousand years, and a
thousand years are like a day. The Lord is not slow
in keeping his promise, as some understand slowness.
Instead, he is patient with you, not wanting anyone
to perish, but everyone to come to repentance.
II Peter 3:8-9

Press In

That person is like a tree planted by streams
of water, which yields its fruit in season
and whose leaf does not wither and
whatever they do prospers.
Psalms 1:3

EBERHARD GROSSGAS

I'm really nothing special. Just an average gal living in the Midwest. What DOES make me special? The redeeming blood of Jesus. My desire to fulfill this call. I've ran from it. I've asked God to take it away. Have tried to sabotage it. The best part about this? God is faithful...even when we're not. His call is irrevocable. He knows what we're capable of. He knows the talent He has equipped us with. He knows our boundaries. Our shortcomings. Our worst fears...and our heart's desire.

Let's take this even further. I quit going to church for several years. Didn't want to go. Been hurt enough. Stepped on. Pushed away. Made to feel 'less than' valuable. But the real reason is probably this: If I didn't show up, then I could better ignore the call. There. You have it. I was running.

Please read very intently. Allow your heart to 'listen' very closely. The call He lovingly places on our life isn't for us. It's for others. We are to be the guide. The arrow, if you will, to point others in the right direction. Be salt. Be light. Be love.

As you can probably tell, as you hold this book in your hands, my days of running are over. I am learning to FULLY embrace this unique gifting of 'restoration'. Restoring what, you ask? Inviting someone to receive the gift of salvation. Talking with them about their value, and His deep and sincere love for them.

Explaining the cleansing power of the blood of Jesus. It is powerful. Brings hope. Strips demonic oppression. Offers eternal security. Life changing it is.

He offers deep roots to those that trust Him. He offers living water to those of us that are thirsty. He offers rest, and to take the heavy burden upon Himself. And…He offers a home with Him in Heaven, and for eternity.

♥ PRESS IN. Don't run. Answer His knock. He's been knocking at your heart's door for a long time. Are you ready to answer? Choose Him! He's already chosen you.

_____

_____

_____

_____

Passionate

For the LORD is good.
His unfailing love continues forever,
and his faithfulness continues to each generation.
Psalm 100:5

In John 21, we read the story of Jesus asking Peter three times, "Simon, son of Jonah, do you love Me?". Peter answers, "Yes, Lord, you know that I love you." Jesus then says, "Then feed my sheep." It hit me just how PASSIONATE Jesus was about His calling in life. He was not a man nor a Savior to be found passive in any way. He knew who He was and what His game plan was. He didn't waste time on things that didn't matter. We never found Him in fear, never backing away from responsibility, never out of touch with His beloved disciples and followers. As I was studying John 20 and 21, I noticed the phrase "and the other disciple, the one whom Jesus loved". Get ready for this little nugget of "amazingness". This is John speaking of HIMSELF! The Lord had a special way about Him to make others feel deeply loved and valued. It's a bit humorous to know John tucked this golden phrase into scripture for us! You see., Jesus was such a wonderful 'people' person, dear friend, and leader that John was convinced he was loved above all! My Lord....You are amazing! Always showing us in scripture that You were, and still are, in the business of RESTORATION...and RELATIONSHIP BUILDING. We can see lovingly scattered throughout scripture that He was also in the business of HEALING LIVES and MENDING BROKEN HEARTS.

In a spiritual nutshell, Jesus was PASSIONATE about every single person His life touched. Whether He was restoring Peter to complete fellowship with Him or beckoning him onward to so Peter could fulfill the call on his life of "feed my sheep". Another beautiful example of His love...His gesture of asking that His mother be taken care of while He was enduring the Cross. And then there is the woman with the issue of blood 'merely' touching the very hem of His garment. He felt the healing power leave Him as she reached out for Him.

He was so PASSIONATELY FOCUSED on those that He loved. He was, without a doubt, IN TUNE with those around Him. He purposed to know them. He purposed to make a difference...and a difference He certainly made. He chose the Cross knowing the pain He would endure. A passionate man. A purposeful Savior with a burning desire to reconcile those He loved with His Heavenly Father. The plan worked beautifully and continues to this day.

"Father, dial my heart's focus in very clearly and closely to You. Let my purpose and passion be crystal clear and may I wrap my arms and heart around those that I encounter in my life to point them towards You, and Your purpose for them. Lord God, may my life glorify You ~ even through down times may my lips sing glory to Your name. May I be assured knowing that You restore and revive us over and over again. When I turn left, help me to turn right. When I take steps that back me away from You....guide and direct me, once again, in the direction and purpose You placed on this heart and this life. Amen."

♥ What are you passionately focused on?

_____

_____

_____

_____

_____

_____

_____

_____

_____

_____

_____

_____

_____

_____

_____

_____

_____

_____

Always There

BEN WHITE

Heavenly Father,
I know You're always there
Watching and waiting
Knowing I won't wander far
From my Father's eyes
Your love draws me, O God
Back to You time and time again
I lay down my will
And ask only Your will takes place
Dying to self once again
Over and over again
Trusting and believing
Telling doubt and fear to flee
And gently nuzzling my life
Back into the fold of Your love
And exactly where You intend
For this child to be.

♥ Always there. What do these words mean to you?

_____

_____

_____

_____

_____

_____

_____

_____

_____

_____

_____

_____

_____

_____

Have I not commanded you? Be strong and courageous.
Do not be afraid; do not be discouraged, for the LORD
your God will be with you wherever you go.
Joshua 1:9

Legacy

I press on toward the goal for the prize of the
upward call of God in Christ Jesus.
Philippians 3:14

KEVIN DELVICCHIO

Consider your legacy. What are you preparing to leave your children and grandchildren?

As we get older, we see even more the preciousness of life, and how quickly life goes by. Ecclesiastes 3:2a speaks of "a time to be born and a time to die". Not only do I have a desire to leave my family an inheritance, but I am also leaving prayers they can read long after I have left this world. Prayers prayed over them for years, all my Bible's with every little scribble and date, and hopefully some words of wisdom and a bit of knowledge. Not because I am so wise or even all that knowledgeable, but because my Heavenly Father IS! Every single word written wrapped up in love just for them.

Look within and begin planning your legacy. For one day, all that is truly left of our existence is memories, pictures, words written or spoken to them during this life, the love and time that was shared, and those precious prayers that continue for those we loved.

In closing, join me in praying for our children, grandchildren, great grandchildren, and on and on…until Jesus returns.

♥ How do you feel about leaving a legacy for your family? What would you like to be remembered for?

_____

_____

_____

_____

_____

_____

_____

_____

_____

_____

_____

_____

George Washington

Jesus Christ is the
same yesterday

MARK ALLEN YOUNG

and today and forever.
Hebrews 13:8

Was George Washington a Christian? Consider these words from his personal prayer book and decide: 'Oh, eternal and everlasting God, direct my thoughts, words, and work. Wash away my sins in the immaculate blood of the lamb and purge my heart by the Holy Spirit. Daily, frame me more and more in the likeness of thy son, Jesus Christ, that living in thy fear, and dying in thy favor, I may in thy appointed time obtain the resurrection of the justified unto eternal life. Bless, O Lord, the whole race of mankind and let the world be filled with the knowledge of thy son, Jesus Christ.'

I can see him, in my mind's eye, sitting in his presidential office, writing in his personal prayer book. I found one statement that said, "Throughout his life, he spoke of the value of righteousness, and of seeking and offering thanks for the "blessings of Heaven." George Washington was born in 1732 and died in 1799 at the age of 67. He was born into this world, lived a full and devoted life, and chose to bow his knee to Almighty God recognizing his state of being lost without Him.

The same Heavenly Father that loved and cared for George Washington is the same God that loves and cares for you.

Beautifully Broken

And she made a vow, saying, "LORD Almighty, if you
will only look on your servant's misery and remember
me, and not forget your servant but give her a son,
then I will give him to the LORD for all the days of his
life, and no razor will ever be used on his head."
I Samuel 1:11

I've had Hannah on my mind lately. The Word speaks of
Hannah weeping before God. Have you ever found yourself on
your knees...hot tears streaming down your face and pouring
your heart out to God? Hannah's heart was broken. She prayed
and sincerely believed God for a son...completely broken before
Him. You see.... Hannah was a wife and unable to present her
husband with a child. Hannah....weeping and childless...had
one desire and she laid it out before Him. She knew fully that
her Lord was the One that could provide her the very desire
she longed and prayed for. God did answer her prayers and she
was blessed with a son, Samuel. When she weaned Samuel, she
then dedicated him completely to the Lord's service. I find it so
humbling to know that she prayed, she believed, she received
the desire of her heart and THEN she lovingly opened her arms
completely to give that same gift of her son right back to her
Lord. What an example she gave!

I must admit, as a mother, that it's difficult to think of giving
up time with my children. It's just natural to want to HOLD
ON to them. Even when they're grown. My son, Ross, enlisted
as a Marine. There was a time that I had to hug him goodbye
and send him to a country far away from the comforts and safety
of home. I admit.... I didn't want to. I wanted to hold on and

keep him close. Through my inner struggle with this, it came to me that HE loved my children long before I even knew them. And He loved me enough to share them with me. What an honor. What a huge blessing.

Lord, I can't fully understand Hannah's sacrifice, but I certainly thank You for her example. Help me to have a heart like Hannah. Lord, I want to thank You for unselfishly sending Your own Son to be beautifully broken for us. His sacrifice has brought us an open path and door to You.

♥ Are you a parent? Have you ever felt the way I did? Are you praying to become a parent? I encourage you to pour your heart out below like Hannah did. God honored her prayer of faith. If He would do this for Hannah, He can do it for you.

_____

_____

_____

_____

_____

_____

_____

_____

_____

Above The Fray

Even youths grow tired and weary, and
young men stumble and fall;
but those who hope in the LORD will renew their strength.
They will soar on wings like eagles; they
will run and not grow weary,
they will walk and not be faint.
Isaiah 40:30-31

FRANK MCKENNA

My former boss, Weldon, once said to me..."always stay above the fray". I researched the meaning of "above the fray" because I wanted to clearly understand the meaning. "Above the fray" means "to not let the chaos or hubbub surrounding you affect you."

If we go to the Word, we can find many examples of people that stayed 'above the fray'. Jesus was the very best at this, and probably our best example of staying above it all. Only once did he seem to lose his cool...and even then...He didn't sin. These were his actions in the temple. Think about all his actions.

He cared deeply. He continually sacrificed His time and His energy. He always guided towards truth. He always sought the will of His Father...not selfishly demanding His own will. He planned and He certainly stayed "above the fray" even though the hubbub and drama were always around Him.

One very specific scene grabs my heart...being amid a crowd of people, pushing and pulling at him from all sides. One very ill, but desperate and determined woman was able to touch not only His garment but His heart. The moment she reached out... in her weakness but possessing great faith...the Word says, virtue left Jesus. Among all these people pulling on him...and pressing him.... He was ABOVE THE FRAY and KNEW the power had left Him and poured out towards someone that needed His help. One commentary I read tonight said, "Whatever the problem, weakness or infirmity we face, Jesus is touched by it. Our High Priest Jesus Christ is not only touched by our infirmities but is moved with compassion to meet our needs, redeem our messes and solve our problems." Isn't THAT awesome news? He is MOVED WITH COMPASSION to meet our needs... REDEEMS US from our messes and He LONGS to solve our problems. We can look throughout scripture and see promise after promise of what He desires for us. So many of us grew up on a religious diet of "Hell, Fire and Brimstone" that we need to now allow the Holy Spirit to refocus us and help us to finally understand fully His mercy, His grace, and His forgiveness.

When life gets tough....and it does.... when there is 'hubbub' all around...and there is.... may we CHOOSE to rise 'ABOVE THE FRAY". The Word speaks of mounting up on wings as eagles.... get a FULL picture of that!!! Eagles simply S-O-A-R. That's what they KNOW to do. They don't try...they just do it naturally. Lord God, help us to spread our wings of faith as we learn to abide in Your 'nest' of salvation, security, and assurance of eternity. Help us to live the way You did and to love the way You do.

♥ What is holding you back or even holding you down? Do you need to rise above the fray? Choose to SOAR today, and not let the circumstances of life keep you down. Your obedience to Him and your happiness MATTER!

_____

_____

_____

_____

_____

_____

_____

_____

_____

_____

_____

_____

_____

_____

_____

_____

An Outstretched Hand

Asa's heart was fully committed to the Lord, all his life.
2 Chronicles 15:17b

Father, remind me of a heart being "fully committed". That place where my head stops thinking so much and my heart yields. The place where the loss of something or someone in my life isn't nearly as painful if I can just tap into the faith in my heart and carefully...slowly...push through...realizing the incredible future you have waiting ahead. For weeks, my hands have held on tightly to what I wanted, but the Lord clearly said, "LET GO". "But, Lord, I can't see past tomorrow.... I'm having a difficult time trusting Your word though I know You've always been faithful." In 2 Chronicles notice that Asa's heart was fully committed.... all his life. In Matthew 6:33, we are encouraged to seek first His kingdom and His righteousness, and ALL these things will be added unto us. What is the definition of "ALL" to you? Peace? Forgiveness? A companion? A family? Health? Every one of us have an "ALL" definition. My very favorite scripture and one that I cling to is Psalm 37:4 "Delight yourself in the Lord and He will give you the desires of your heart." This scripture just seems a companion to Matthew 6:33. He has given us SO many promises that I wonder how, truly, do we find ourselves ever feeling alone.... empty.... forgotten.... unforgiven? We've all been there. My Mother used to say there's never a "utopia" but, for some reason, I've always felt there was to be found.... within our own heart.... fully committed for life to the very One that knows us so completely. It's not about a church or the pew you sit in every week. It's not about a denomination.

It's this ongoing, beautiful walk between here and Heaven that holds us close…and together during the good times and the bad.

"Father, I choose to cast all my cares on You for You care for me. I believe, by faith, in Your perfect work and Your perfect will. Tomorrow is a new day, and Your word says Your mercies are NEW every morning. Clean slate. Fresh start. Healed heart and an outstretched hand reaching for You instead of holding onto something that You've lovingly whispered, 'let go'. Make it easier to understand, Lord. Help any loss in my life to make sense to my heart. Allow the sun to shine again and remind me, once more, the depth of Your love and the total and unfathomable depth of Your understanding of any loss, in this life, we experience. Amen."

♥ Rewrite the above paragraph (shown in *Italics*) and make it your very own.

_____

_____

_____

_____

_____

_____

_____

_____

_____

_____

Boxing Shadows

Whoever dwells in the shelter of the Most High will rest
in the shadow of the Almighty. I will say of the Lord, He
is my refuge and my fortress, my God, in whom I trust.
Psalm 91:1-2

Life can certainly throw us a punch. Ever find yourself
backed up in a corner and boxing at dark shadows? One shadow
might be named Fear. Fear...that ugly shadow that rears its nasty
head and causes you to lose your center. Typically, the closest
companion of Fear is his partner "What If....". He causes you
to question and doubt and imagine. Another shadow might be
named Abandonment. That irrational shadow has been allowed
to linger for much too long. Continually taking you back and
echoing past wounds replaying them like a broken record.
Depression. That scroungy dog waiting to pounce upon your
heart and nerves at your weakest moments. What about Loss?
That underlying voice that says you'll always lose those you
love. Over and over...boxing shadows.... a jab to the left.... a jab
to the right.

There IS good news for us. A shining light at the end of a
dark tunnel. A glimmer of hope against a dark corner full of
musty shadows. God's Word, once again, brings us supernatural
comfort. One of my very favorite scripture passages is Psalm 91.
Verse 1 and 2 says "Whoever dwells in the shelter of the Most
High will rest in the shadow of the Almighty. I will say of the
Lord, He is my refuge and my fortress, my God, in whom I
trust."

Find, with me, that amazing and comforting promise in
verse 1. "Whoever" dwells... or places themselves...in the shelter

of the Most High. See it? We will rest in HIS shadow. The SHADOW of the Almighty, our peace, our deliverer, our refuge and the One who wants to be our fortress. There will be no boxing shadows of fear, abandonment, or loss in 'that' place. His word says we will rest. There is no fighting or even losing the battle. We simply can rest...and trust... protected by our loving Father. Our promise is clear. He will never leave us, nor will He ever abandon us. No more boxing empty, powerless shadows for the fight has already been called. The winner has already been named.

♥ Where is your refuge? Where do you go for comfort?

_____

_____

_____

_____

_____

_____

_____

_____

May your unfailing love be my comfort, according to
Your promise to your servant.
Psalm 119:76

Dive In

Forget the former things; do not dwell on the past. See, I am doing a new thing! Now it springs up; do you not perceive it? I am making a way in the desert and streams in the wasteland.
Isaiah 43:18–19

ANIKA MIKKELSON

The Holy Spirit spoke to my heart last night to say, "Why do you continue to wade in a river when you can swim in the ocean?". What the Lord plans for us is so much bigger, so much wider, and much deeper than we could begin to dream. When you are in a place in life that everywhere you turn a door gets closed in your face then maybe it is high time to move forward and test new waters....as He leads. Sometimes we allow ourselves to remain because we're in a comfort zone and don't want to make a change. Sometimes we're miserable within this comfort zone but wrongly determined we must remain. No! The Lord says He is doing a new thing! He is making a way in the dry deserts of our life and preparing the wastelands of our heart to enjoy a new, fresh infilling of His Spirit. Indeed...forget the former things and do not dwell on them any longer. Dive into the ocean of the fantastic future He has planned for you!

♥ Ever find yourself fighting for something that is LESS THAN what God wants for you? May we choose His path, where we can live in peace.

_____

_____

_____

_____

_____

_____

_____

_____

_____

_____

_____

_____

_____

The Kingdom of God

Seek ye first the kingdom of God and His
righteousness and all these things
shall be added unto you.
Matthew 6:33

ANDREAS WEILGUNY

"The Kingdom". His Holy presence. His desire to protect us. His provision to provide for us. He simply says.... seek. The Kingdom of God is the very glue that we need to hold it all together. Within this Kingdom are many rooms. Rooms filled with so many things.... peace for one. Nothing can offer us peace like He can. With Him, we have it. Without Him, we may never experience peace the way He longs for us to experience it. We can walk around and think we have it all together and realize that we have avoided Him for too long. He is a loving and, yes, jealous God. He won't share us for long. His gentle, loving and Heavenly Hand will reach us and guide us back again and again.

"His righteousness". Only He could have made us righteous. Placing his stretched arms across a wooden Cross and willingly laying the foundation for our future. He purchased us with every drop of His blood.... knowing the pain, accepting the temporary separation.... then knowing He had fully paid the price; He took His last breath. Remember that His Father had a divine plan for us. Our value to Him is immeasurable and His love for us is never.... ever.... ending.

"All these things". Don't give me material things that will burn to dust in an instant. Give me a future that is so full of His directive Spirit. Give me the knowing of the Comforter being RIGHT beside me. Give me the KNOWING that I am following, and right in the middle of, His will...and certainly not my own.

"Shall be added". That's a promise. Read the scripture again. Seek first - His Kingdom - His righteousness and ALL these things shall be added....TO YOU.

♥ How can you begin today to seek His kingdom? What do you need to do to start on the road to a closer walk with Him?

_____

_____

_____

_____

_____

_____

Permission Granted

Neither height nor depth, nor anything else in
all creation, will be able to separate us from the
love of God that is in Christ Jesus our Lord.
Romans 8:39

Today is a new day. A new day to give yourself
PERMISSION to be happy. Bottom line. We all make
mistakes. We've all been hurt, wounded, scarred, bruised,
abandoned, left high and dry and today is the day to stop the
madness and realize it is the first day of the rest of our lives. I
know too many people that are still hurting from things that
happened to them YEARS ago (admitting I've resembled
this in the past, too) BUT NO MORE! It's time to draw
your line in the sand and say, "I AM GONNA BE HAPPY!"
Quit worrying about what other people think. Quit finding
more comfort in sad tears than tears of joy. I'm reminded of
attending a divorce recovery class in approximately 2002. I
was sitting in this big room with a large circle of women of
all ages. Many were crying and very upset. I started crying,
too, because the oppression was just so heavy in the room.
I'm thinking "maybe this is a good thing.... cleansing...
healing.... bring it on!?" and then several of the women
began to talk about their divorce. Some had been divorced
for 5 years, 10 years and one for even 35 years!!!!! OH,
MY GOODNESS!! God has HEALING for our hearts. We
absolutely were not created to carry around burdens that
bend our shoulders down below our knees (and it looks kind
of weird, too, walking like that!). We just aren't built to
function that way. A friend of mine told me one day that he

advises his clients, when they are carrying much guilt, that he's going to place a backpack on them and weigh it down with heavy rocks. Eventually, he said, he knew they would get tired of 'carrying the weight' and finally lay it down. So... guess what? TODAY is the day to take off your backpack of rocks and lay them down. My question is where in the world did, we get the idea we are supposed to feel guilty and condemned all the time? Things in my past that I have confessed (I John 1:9) are now as far from the east is from the west. (Ps 103:12) There is VICTORY, and we no longer need to be a victim of 1) ourselves 2) others 3) past mistakes or 4) future challenges. Shake it off like a dirty suit! Awhile back I wrote a devotion called "Glory Suit". That is what I encourage us with today is that we place our 'glory suit' on and know that, YES, we will mess up sometimes, but may we never allow GUILT or CONDEMNATION or FEAR or SORROW or ANGER or ANYTHING keep us from experiencing the FULL joy of our SALVATION and our life.

Have you had a vacation lately? Well....I think it's high time you sit down and decide what you can do this week to make yourself H-A-P-P-Y!! My son, Ross, made the comment to me last night about 'living on my happy cloud'. Well, it's just TRUE! Understand that no one will make you happy.... it's your job.... with the help of the Holy Spirit. PULL your 'happy cloud' out from inside of your very own heart and LIVE!!

PERMISSION GRANTED THIS DAY to be GLORIOUSLY HAPPY!

♥ What does your HAPPY CLOUD look like today?

_____

_____

_____

_____

_____

_____

_____

_____

_____

_____

_____

_____

_____

_____

_____

_____

_____

_____

The Bridge

MODESTAS URBONAS

This devotion is a reminder that our Father in Heaven is still in the business of building and reconstruction. He is the very best at making our crooked roads straight again. All he asks for is a willing heart. During these times of 'heart renovation' He allows our hearts to be hollowed out so that He can rebuild and refill us with the healing power of His Holy Spirit. He allows issues within us to be exposed so that we can be regenerated and renewed restoring our hope, joy, and fellowship with Him. Going through the process isn't so glorious, but the process is both necessary and well worth the journey.

Disappointment can push you into the wrong place in life. It can cause you to make choices you wouldn't normally make, and to do things you wouldn't normally do, and be someone God never intended you to be. Disappointment can distract you and cause you to want to give up...BUT THEN GOD... He always has a bridge to reconnect your heart to Him. He's working in the very midst of every disappointment in your life... no matter how large or how small. He's building a foundation;

he's stretching far and wide across your devastation to bridge you right back to Him.

Catch a glimpse of the Father looking down the road at His prodigal child. Keep your eyes and heart straight ahead and cross that bridge He's built for you. You're almost home.

Manipulation No More

Do not take advantage of each other but fear
your God. I am the LORD your God.
I Thessalonians 4:6

This is your heads up to manipulation. Do NOT let anyone manipulate you. Your life is yours. Other people may not like your decisions or your actions, but it is YOUR LIFE. God takes care of us in His way and on His timeline. Trust Your Heavenly Father to bring you what you need when you need it. Do not let someone else tell you what you must have, or what you must walk away from. SEE CLEARLY THROUGH YOUR OWN EYES and take your next steps towards freedom and FAR FROM manipulation.

♥ Look up the definition of manipulation. Become familiar with what it is. Then determine to not allow yourself to be manipulated, nor manipulate others.

_____

_____

_____

_____

_____

_____

_____

Banish Fear

So do not fear, for I am with you; do not be dismayed,
for I am your God. I will strengthen you and help you;
I will uphold you with my righteous right hand.
Isaiah 41:10

"Fear is a powerful tool until facts get in the way". FEAR
paralyzes. FEAR cripples. FEAR is a thief of precious moments.
FEAR is a liar. FEAR is not your friend. The Word says, "We
were not given a spirit of fear, but of POWER, of LOVE, and
a SOUND MIND."

Imagine placing your fear into a box today. Then cast this
box full of fear FAR FROM YOU. It is not yours...and it never
was. When you realize the fact that you are an OVERCOMER,
then you will learn fear has NO POWER over you. When you
realize that you are a child of the King...then fear can hold you
NO MORE. When you begin exposing truth and light...then
fear falls away.

♥ **Write below:** "For God has not given us a spirit of fear,
but of power and of love and of a sound mind." 2 Timothy
1:7. I encourage you to memorize this verse.

_____

_____

_____

_____

The Dream is Real

Do you not know? Have you not heard? The Lord
is the everlasting God the Creator of the ends
of the earth. He will not grow tired or weary,
and His understanding no one can fathom.
Isaiah 40:28

What is your dream? Write it down. Take it to our Heavenly
Father. Listen. Watch as He lovingly unfolds His plan. He's
never early. He's never late. He's always right on time.

♥ Share your dream(s). Prioritize them if you need to!

_____

_____

_____

_____

_____

_____

_____

_____

_____

_____

The Creative Mind of God

I have been crucified with Christ and I no longer live, but Christ lives in me. The life I live in the body, I live by faith in the Son of God, who loved me and gave himself for me.
Galatians 2:20

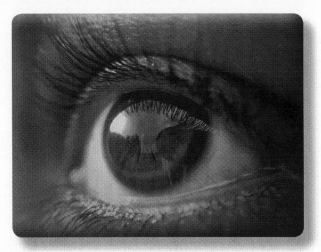

SWAPNIL POTDAR

Have you ever heard someone make the comment, "I don't believe God is interested in the little things in my life?" Let me expound on a few little details of just how interested He truly is. Let's consider the fact that 50,000 of the cells in your body will die and be replaced with new cells, all while you're reading this sentence! A plan for regeneration of our cells and blood! Did you know He designed your left lung smaller than your right lung to make room for your heart? What a loving Father to hollow out a very special place for our heart!

Consider that He knew our eyes needed protection from dust, so He designed the lid to blink to protect our eyes. The average person blinks approximately 23,040 times a day or 6.25 million times in a year. Lastly, did you know that eight (8) weeks after a baby is conceived every little organ is in place, the bones begin to replace cartilage, their little fingerprints begin to form, and a baby can begin to hear? What a miraculous, artistic way of showing His love even from the very beginning!

As you can see God is, INDEED, very interested in the little things. He's also interested in the condition of your heart and soul, he's concerned about the state of your mind and all other decisions that He would be glad to be a part of. Invite Him into your every single day. Talk to Him about the details of your life. Praise Him today for His grand design of Y-O-U! Remember that before you were a twinkle (or a blink) in your parents' eyes, He already had a beautiful, original design with your very name carved upon it.

Father, thank You for Your creative mind that was thinking of us all along. Help us to know You more, deep within our hearts, to see Your face and understand You more clearly...Lord, we want to know You more. Amen.

♥ Do you love knowing that God is interested in the details of your life? He even stores our tears in Heaven. He doesn't dismiss our tears. He is our caring, and intimate God of details.

_____

_____

_____

_____

_____

_____

_____

_____

_____

_____

_____

_____

_____

_____

_____

_____

_____

_____

_____

_____

You keep track of all my sorrows. You have
collected all my tears in your bottle.
You have recorded each one in your book.
Psalm 56:8

His Masterpiece

He has made everything beautiful in its time. He has
also set eternity in the hearts of men; yet they cannot
fathom what God has done from beginning to end.
Ecclesiastes 3:11

ENZO TOMMASI

There's a country song that says, "don't you know you're
beautiful just the way you are". It is amazing to me how many
people are so hard on themselves. They criticize every little part
of themselves.

We need to understand this. He knit us, according to Psalm 139, in our mother's womb. Amazing!! Realize today that no one in the world has the exact same sparkle in their eyes as you do. Look at your fingertips and realize also that the God of all creation loved you so much He made a one-of-a-kind pattern for your very own fingerprints...never to be duplicated again. Look at that beautiful smile on your face, knowing that no one smiles just like you do! The tone of your voice, the touch of your hand, the way you walk, the gifts placed within you.... are uniquely you.

YOU ARE HIS MASTERPIECE! He not only made you special, but He also made a special way for you to be in fellowship with Him. If you've never experienced that wonderful washing of your spirit, that washing away that takes place when you hand over all your heartache and disappointments.... those things that make us feel less than enough...let today be THAT day. I John 1:9 says, "If you confess your sins, He is faithful to forgive you and cleanse you of all unrighteousness." It is so very simple. Give to Him the very things He's already paid for. You no longer must carry them. You were never meant to carry them. Let today be the day that you accept yourself just the way you are and accept Him fully for who HE is.

COME ON! Let those gorgeous eyes twinkle...that extraordinary smile beam across your face...and just bask in the beautiful truth that not only are you so VERY lovable but also that He loves you so very much! Your heart can rest always in the palm of His hand. He is faithful and trustworthy. He is the glorious Artist and Creator that will never fail you.... His precious Masterpiece!

♥ Did you know there is only ONE YOU! You ARE a masterpiece! How does this make you feel to know that He designed you so very special?

_____

_____

_____

_____

_____

_____

_____

_____

_____

_____

_____

_____

_____

_____

_____

_____

_____

_____

Are You Ready?

The Lord is my rock and my fortress and my deliverer,
my God, my rock, in whom I take refuge,
my shield, and the horn of my salvation,
my stronghold.
Psalms 18:2

In the days we are now living, today is a perfect day to trust in the Lord. Allow Him to be your rock. If He is truly your rock, HE is who you turn to instead of the media or news reports. As we choose to trust Him, fear will fall away. Doubt will disappear. Anxiety will be diminished. Why? Because you are NOW standing in the shadow of the Most High. Trusting Him…and looking to Him is what matters most. He IS and will continue to be the calm in any storm you ever face. Are you ready?

♥ Write Psalms 18:2 below. Choose to make Him your rock, fortress, and deliverer.

_____

_____

_____

_____

_____

_____

The New You

Let your eyes look straight ahead; fix your gaze
directly before you. Give careful thought to the paths
for your feet and be steadfast in all your ways.
Proverbs 4:25–26

MOHAMED NOHASSI

The NEW you. Not the former wounded you.... the one that family or friends were so accustomed to seeing and hearing from. Here's the deal. Over time, we heal. And we grow. And we come to a time of truly knowing ourselves better. We know what we like...and what we don't. We know what helps us to soar and what clips our wings. We learn to step into our power and not allow it to be smothered and taken away by others.

A great example was Paul, the former Saul. He was struck down in a moment, and then shown the new path he would be on the rest of his life. Reminder that his former reputation was one of torturing Christians. He was known to beat, imprison and have believers killed due to their faith in Jesus. After his conversion, how could others know he had truly changed? He had been widely feared and now...he was a changed man? It took TIME for them to see this change in him. It took his confession of faith. It took a changed, contrite heart and one that dedicated the rest of his life to the very One that changed him.

And THAT is the key...it takes TIME. It takes FAITH. So, allow yourself time to develop your character, deepen your integrity and know fully your worth. Allow God's Word to build your confidence in Him.

♥ How do you see yourself? How does God see you according to His Word?

_____

_____

_____

_____

_____

_____

_____

_____

_____

_____

Be Kind

Be kind to one another, tenderhearted, forgiving
one another, as God in Christ forgave you.
Ephesians 4:32

"After all, it is only when mean people actually are happy and free from suffering that they will stop trying to take us down with them." (Author Unknown)

NOW THAT IS A WISE THOUGHT. I believe the only way to deal with mean-spirited people is to be kind. For some reason... and only they know why...they are just miserable. Even when you confront them...they have no idea how to respond. THESE people, indeed, need the most love and compassion. Consider King Saul and David. No matter how David tried to rise above the manure of how King Saul treated him, David remained pure in heart towards him and even when he had the opportunity to take Saul's life...did not. May we learn from this example.

♥ Do you have mean spirited people in your life? Pray for them. Do you ever think you might be mean spirited? If so, repent below, and ask God to fill you with compassion and kindness.

_____

_____

_____

_____

Baby Steps

I've kept my feet on the ground,
I've cultivated a quiet heart.
Like a baby content in its mother's arms,
my soul is a baby content.
Psalm 131:2

THE VERY thing that breaks you is what can begin to rebuild you. Your heart can be broken, you can lose your way, you can feel it is all over…. but SOMETHING IS BORN in your soul….and you begin taking baby steps towards healing. You may find, as you stretch out your arms in the darkest moments, that you will discover your best friend. YOU.

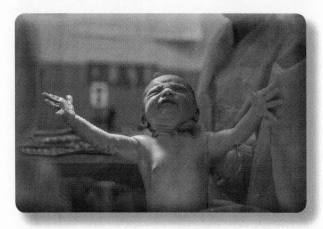

ALEX HOCKETT

Real

For you were once darkness but are now light in the Lord.
Live as children of light.
Ephesians 5:8

Give me REAL. Every single time. Those of us that have seen a glimpse of the darkness through depression or anxiety or addiction...and lived through it...we know real. We also know the lack of real. We were never called to be perfect during this journey. We were called to be salt and light. From an Abram to an Abraham. From a Sarai to a Sarah. Lessons learned. Maturity in the Spirit happens. Our journey towards healing continues.

♥ Are you real? Think deeply about this. Ask God to help you see clearly who you really are. Don't allow any deception to shadow who you truly are to the core of you.

_____

_____

_____

_____

_____

_____

_____

The Power of Words

A person's words can be life-giving
water, words of true wisdom
are as refreshing as a bubbling brook.
Proverbs 18:4

Powerful words. We are all human. We fail each other and ourselves. Today, may we be reminded of every word that leaves our mouths. Do they build up? Or tear down? Yes. We have been given that power.

♥ Write Psalms 35:28 below. "My tongue will proclaim your righteousness, your praises all day long." As we focus more on Him, and grow our character accordingly, our mouths should also line up. Our words matter!

_____

_____

_____

_____

_____

_____

_____

_____

Watch and Listen

Love is patient and kind; love does not envy or boast;
it is not arrogant or rude. It does not insist on its own
way; it is not irritable or resentful; it does not rejoice at
wrongdoing but rejoices with the truth. Love bears all things,
believes all things, hopes all things, endures all things.
I Corinthians 13:4-7

People will provoke you until they bring out your ugly side,
then play victim when you go there. We've all experienced this.
A bully will poke, prod, and provoke. When you stand up for
yourself…it's a different story then.

People show you who they are. Just watch and listen.

NICK FEWINGS

No More Regrets

Forget the former things; do not dwell on the
past. See, I am doing a new thing! Now it springs
up; do you not perceive it? I am making a way in
the wilderness and streams in the wasteland.
Isaiah 43:18,19

Regrets. Let them GO. We must have an understanding that
we cannot go back and change the past. If we allow regrets to
continue to plague us, it is counterproductive for our emotional
and spiritual health. Walk away and leave it FAR BEHIND you.

We can move towards a wonderful future! Pull that heavy
bag of regret off your shoulders today.

♥ Do you have regrets in your life that you need to place at the
foot of the Cross? Do that today. Write them down below,
or on a separate page if needed, and LET THEM GO!

_____

_____

_____

_____

_____

_____

Survival

Delight yourself in the Lord and He will
give you the desires of your heart.
Psalms 37:4

If you are reading this...YOU HAVE SURVIVED. Your mother carried you and, at some point, you entered this world. Place your arms around yourself and give yourself a big hug. Then take a good look in the mirror and remind yourself that you are still living and breathing. AND IF YOU ARE...there is HOPE for a bright future! There is breath within your lungs to get you from one day to the next. You have survived your best days...and your worst days.

I encourage you to continue this beautiful path. Set goals for your future and determine just what you want your life to look like. LOOK UP and begin asking for what you want in this life. He's listening!

♥ You are a survivor! Write a note to YOU and tell yourself how proud you are to have survived every day up to now! HE HAS A PLAN FOR YOU!

_____

_____

_____

_____

_____

Power, Love, & A Sound Mind

So do not fear, for I am with you; do not
be dismayed, for I am your God.
I will strengthen you and help you; I will uphold
you with my righteous right hand."
Isaiah 41:10

"Fear is a powerful tool until facts get in the way". FEAR paralyzes. FEAR cripples. FEAR is a thief of precious moments. FEAR is a liar. FEAR is not your friend. The Word says, "We were not given a spirit of fear, but of POWER, of LOVE, and a SOUND MIND."

Imagine placing your fear into a box today. Then cast this box full of fear FAR FROM YOU. It is not yours...and it never was. When you realize the fact that you are an OVERCOMER, then you will learn fear has NO POWER over you. When you realize that you are a child of the King...then fear can hold you NO MORE. When you begin exposing truth and light...then fear falls away.

I remember when fear and depression tried to overtake my life. IT DID NOT! Stand up on your own two feet and declare THIS IS YOUR DAY! FEAR no longer has a hold on you.

♥ Write the scripture shown under the title. I encourage you to research fear and faith. You will realize fear has NO POWER over you UNLESS you allow it!

_____

_____

_____

_____

_____

_____

_____

_____

_____

_____

_____

_____

_____

_____

_____

_____

_____

Winds of Change

KHAMEO VILAYSING

Then Daniel praised the God of heaven and said: "Praise be
to the name of God forever and ever; wisdom and power
are his. He changes times and seasons; he sets up kings and
deposes them. He gives wisdom to the wise and knowledge to
the discerning. He reveals deep and hidden things; he knows
what lies in darkness, and light dwells with him. I thank and
praise you, O God of my fathers: You have given me wisdom
and power, you have made known to me what we asked of
you, you have made known to us the dream of the king.
Daniel 2:20-23

I can feel it. It's in my soul. Winds of change are coming.
Things are not going to stay the way they've always been. There
will be crucial changes and necessary changes.

Reality check regarding change. Look in the mirror and
see the image before you. That person will be with you every
day. THAT is a guarantee. The question is whether that person

you see is ready for the change that is coming. It's just life. Hearts change. People change. Homes change. Jobs change. The question is do you truly want things to stay the way they've always been? That 'wheel' in your life that just spins and goes seemingly nowhere? Listen.… truth brings liberation from ties that bind. Truth reveals the darkness in our hearts that must be filtered out and allow new luminosity to expose how life should really be. Our hearts were never meant to be placed within a set of unyielding vise grips. Our hearts were created to soar!

That leaves us with simply this.… all that matters is what truly matters. Where are you? Who are you? Living for others or opening your whole heart to what God wants to show you? Life is such an amazing adventure that surely, we don't want to be stuck on the side of the road in a ditch. Don't allow roadblocks of bitterness or anger to push you off the course. Stay your course and continue your journey towards blue skies that are clear, a heart that is pure and a mind that is not buried in uncertainty.

Today, feel the winds of change are coming and welcome them with open arms. Life will never be the same.

♥ Are you ready for positive change in your life?

_____

_____

_____

_____

_____

_____

Safe Harbor

Then they cried out to the Lord in their trouble;
He delivered them out of their distresses.
Psalms 107:6

◊ TRAUMA HAPPENS. The most hurtful part of trauma is when our story is not trusted, is misaligned, or not believed.

◊ May we all have a safe harbor in the presence of those that will honor our vulnerability and resilience to heal.

◊ In time, we do heal. Having a strong support system in place is vital to help us along our healing journey.

♥ Do you have a support system in place? There are so many wonderful resources for support including family, friends, support groups, church groups, even Facebook has avenues for emotional and spiritual support. God is ultimate your safe harbor!

_____

_____

_____

_____

_____

_____

_____

The Grand Performance

Thank You, Father,
That the greatest victories I've seen
Have come out of struggles fought
Within my own heart
When there's just You and me.
Deliverance performed by Your Almighty Hand
When there's no parting of waters
Or great speeches or applause
Just the quietness of You moving
Within the depths of my heart...
That part placed within me
That continues to seek
A little peace, a little calm
A little joy and a little balance.
Thank You, Father,
That You are quietly molding me
By a Grand Performance
Wrought by Your Loving Hands
With a Heavenly Promise
That You will be faithful to complete
What You first began.

ELIZABETH WALES

♥ What victories have you seen rise out of the ashes of your struggles?

_____

_____

_____

_____

_____

_____

_____

_____

_____

_____

_____

_____

_____

_____

_____

_____

_____

Lift My Eyes

I lift up my eyes to the hills ~ where
does my help come from?
My help comes from the Lord, the
Maker of heaven and earth.
Psalms 121:1-2

FROM MY JOURNAL

Every single day I am growing stronger

The blood pumps through this strong heart within me

It has carried me through so many things

And I know it will not fail me now

I lift my eyes to the Heavens

As I feel the strength and power underneath me

Surrounding me with the many gifts I have been given

This woman knows who she is

And she knows she'll never lose herself again.

♥ THINK ABOUT IT: "Never lose herself again". What do these words mean to you?

_____

_____

_____

_____

_____

_____

_____

_____

_____

_____

_____

_____

_____

_____

_____

_____

See Beyond The Natural

For God so loved the world that he gave his
one and only Son, that whoever believes
in him shall not perish but have eternal life.
John 3:16

MARINA VITALE

For as long as I can remember...I have walked into places and seen souls. Every single person has one. And a heart. If we knew their story ~ if they knew ours...things in this world would be much different.

May we always have eyes that see beyond the natural. Beyond the outer layer that surrounds them. At times, hear beyond the words they speak and know that there is a soul deep inside of them wanting to be heard and understood.

"If only our eyes saw souls instead of bodies, how
different our ideas of beauty would be."
Lauren Jauregui

♥ Allow your own eyes to begin seeing others spiritual need for Jesus. Begin praying for your family and friends to truly know Him. Make a list of those you feel burdened for. Begin praying for each one today. As you are healing, you can see God begin to move in their lives.

_____

_____

_____

_____

_____

_____

_____

_____

_____

_____

_____

_____

_____

_____

_____

Passionate

Then the disciple whom Jesus loved said
to Peter, "It is the Lord!" ...
John 21:7

FUU J

It hit me just how PASSIONATE Jesus was about His calling in life. He was not a man nor a Savior to be found passive in any way. He knew who He was and what His game plan was. He didn't waste time on things that didn't matter. We never found Him in fear, never backing away from responsibility, never out of touch with His beloved disciples and followers. As I was studying John 20 and 21, I noticed the phrase "and the other disciple, the one whom Jesus loved". Get ready for this little nugget of "amazingness". This is John speaking of **HIMSELF**! The Lord had a special way about Him that made others feel deeply loved and valued. It's a bit humorous to know

John tucked this golden phrase into scripture for us! You see, Jesus was such a wonderful 'people' person, dear friend, and leader that John was convinced he was loved above all! My Lord...You are amazing! Always showing us in scripture that You were, and still are, in the business of RESTORATION and RELATIONSHIP BUILDING. We can see lovingly scattered throughout scripture that God was also in the business of HEALING LIVES and MENDING BROKEN HEARTS.

In a spiritual nutshell, Jesus was PASSIONATE about every single person His life touched. Whether He was restoring Peter to complete fellowship with Him or beckoning him onward to fulfill the call on his life of "feed my sheep". Another beautiful example of His love...His gesture of asking that His mother be taken care of while He was enduring the Cross. And then there is the woman with the issue of blood 'merely' touching the very hem of His garment. He felt the healing power leave Him as she reached out for Him.

He was so PASSIONATELY FOCUSED on those that He loved. He was, without a doubt, IN TUNE with those around Him. He purposed to know them. He purposed to make a difference...and a difference He certainly made. He chose the Cross knowing the pain He would endure. A passionate man. A purposeful Savior with a burning desire to reconcile those He loved with His Heavenly Father. The plan worked beautifully and continues to this day.

"Father, dial my heart's focus in very clearly and closely to You. Let my purpose and passion be crystal clear and may I wrap my arms and heart around those that I encounter in my life to point them towards You, and Your purpose for them. Lord may my life glorify You ~ even through down times may my lips sing glory to Your name. May I be assured knowing that You restore and revive us over and over again. When I turn left, help me to turn right. When I take steps that back me away from You....guide and direct me, once again, in the direction and purpose You placed on this heart and this life. Amen."

♥ How does it feel to know He loves you with this same passion? We are His bride. We are the focus of His heart. He wants to heal us in every part.

_____

_____

_____

_____

_____

_____

_____

_____

_____

_____

_____

_____

_____

_____

_____

Welcome Peace

For I know the plans I have for you," declares the
Lord, "plans to prosper you and not to harm you,
plans to give you hope and a future. Then you will call
on me and come and pray to me, and I will listen to
you. You will seek me and find me when you seek me
with all your heart. I will be found by you," declares
the Lord, "and will bring you back from captivity.
Jeremiah 29:11-11

So important. Especially those
of us that have had trauma. Choose
peace. Pray. Remember that anxiety
is a fear of the future. Only He holds
the future in His very capable Hands.
We can trust this truth. Jeremiah
29:11-14 is such a promise to cling
to every day.

JEFFERY ERHUNSE

♥ Write out JEREMIAH 29:11-14 below. Thank Him for having your future in His very capable Hands.

_____

_____

_____

_____

_____

_____

_____

_____

_____

_____

_____

_____

_____

_____

_____

_____

Shakespeare Wisdom

The meaning of life is to find your gift.
The purpose of life is to give it away.
~ William Shakespeare

MARCEL ARDIVAN

THAT SHAKESPEARE. Pretty smart guy. Don't you dare keep your gifts to yourself! You have arms ~ **HUG** those that need it. You have lips ~ **SPEAK** positive words over yourself, and over those around you. You have a heart ~ **LOVE** with everything that is within you.

♥ Are you ready to BE love? To accept love? To receive love?

_____

_____

_____

_____

Sitting on the Dock

Therefore I say to you, do not worry about your life,
what you will eat or what you will drink; nor about
your body, what you will put on. Is not life more than
food and the body more than clothing? Look at the birds
of the air, for they neither sow nor reap nor gather into
barns; yet your Heavenly Father feeds them. Are you not
of more value than they? Which of you by worrying
can add one cubit to his stature?"
Matthew 6:25–27

MICHAEL KURZYNOWSKI

Laying in a hammock looking out over the ocean, I noticed
the seagulls hovering over the beach and then landing on the
dock in front of me. I watched as they fluttered around, seeming
to communicate with each other and then calm themselves as
they each found a little place to perch at the very end of the dock.
They were completely still and so peaceful. I watched them......
taking in all the sun, the cool morning breeze and noticed

that they were worried about absolutely nothing.... N-A-D-A. To be a seagull placed in Cozumel. What a beautiful place to be.... surrounded by THE most beautiful azure water, beaming sunshine that seems never ending and all the peace they could possibly want. They weren't worried about the weather, their job, their home, their relationships, their finances, or anything! They were just sitting, peacefully, in all of God's magnificent glory in Cozumel, Mexico. "Lord, remind us that there are no worries to hold within us. Just a place at the dock of our 'bay' to place our fullest trust in You....acknowledging if You take care of these lovely seagulls every day, You will certainly prove Yourself faithful in our lives. You are Jehovah-Jireh, our God who provides. Thank You for the reminder in Your Word of how You deeply care for us, find great value in us and desire that we will trust You in all things. Amen."

♥ What worries do you need to place at the foot of the Cross today?

_____

_____

_____

_____

_____

_____

_____

_____

Creative Messages

There is no one holy like the LORD; there is no one
besides you; there is no Rock like our God.
I Samuel 2:2

OH LORD GOD, you are quite amazing. My heart is so
grateful for the words of wisdom that You send. Just the right
words at the right time. What a blessing to see eyes that 'get it' as
their hearts begin to open. The creative messages that You share
that help precious people to choose life, to extend forgiveness,
to see and grab ahold of a lifeline called hope.... they see how
to finally 'let go' of things they have held on to for years.

Yes....I am so very grateful for Your words and for You being
everything that You are.

♥ Jot down a love letter to Him today…right where you are at.

_____

_____

_____

_____

_____

_____

_____

True North

You have looked deep into my heart, LORD, and you know all about me. You know when I am resting or when I am working, and from heaven you discover my thoughts. You notice everything I do and everywhere I go. Before I even speak a word, you know what I will say, and with your powerful arm you protect me from every side. I can't understand all of this! Such wonderful knowledge is far above me.

Psalm 139: 1-6

JAMIE STREET

TRUE NORTH. What is your TRUE NORTH? It is that place in the deepest part of you that nurtures your soul. It is that voice that whispers...you CAN do this. Your TRUE NORTH is that simple knowing that you are stronger than you think that you are more valuable than you feel...and it is something within you that guides you to another day.

Every single day we can choose to trust that voice. We can choose to be a kinder person, a more loving human being, and we can choose to allow our hearts to be nurtured instead of being sabotaged. CHOOSE YOU.

♥ Where is your true north? What nurtures your soul? Write your favorite scripture below or even the one shown in this devotion.

_____

_____

_____

_____

_____

_____

_____

_____

_____

_____

_____

_____

_____

Not-Enoughness

Look to the LORD and his strength; seek his face always.
I Chronicles 16:11

NOT-ENOUGHNESS ~ That word needs to be expired from your vocabulary. That language, within your own heart, that screams "YOU ARE NOT ENOUGH ~ YOU ARE A FAILURE". NO ma'am! NO sir! You take charge and remove that voice that tries to deplete your power. YOU ARE ENOUGH...AND HAVE ALWAYS BEEN.

♥ Write "I AM ENOUGH. IN HIM, I HAVE ALWAYS BEEN ENOUGH." You are. Begin today embracing how special you are. NO ONE is just like you, dear friend.

_____

_____

_____

_____

_____

_____

_____

_____

Share Your Crown

Praise the LORD, my soul; all my inmost being, praise his
holy name. Praise the LORD, my soul, and forget not all
his benefits—who forgives all your sins and heals all your
diseases, who redeems your life from the pit and crowns you
with love and compassion, who satisfies your desires with
good things so that your youth is renewed like the eagle's.
Psalms 103:1-5

The Spirit showed me something so very clearly. We, as
women and especially as brothers or sisters-in-Christ, should
always be willing to share our crown. We should always want
our friends to win. We should be willing to step up and care
for them. Sometimes that means a meal, a phone call, an offer

JARED SUBIA

to visit. Or maybe even a hand to hold,
and certainly being a friend to pray.

Sharing our crown means we
have a deep awareness that others are
worthy and deserving of love, care, and
understanding from us. There is no time
for nonsense or drama.

We share compassion because He
has already extended it to us…and we
know, without a shadow of a doubt, we
would be nothing without Him. The
anointing…HIS anointing…is so very important.

In the end, we will receive crowns in Heaven to reward us
for a life well-lived. Those same glorious crowns we are given
will then be cast at His feet.

♥ When you fully embrace the beautiful person God created you to be, you will have opportunities to share your own crown. This can include your testimony...your own story of defeat and redemption. Sharing your heart with others and pointing them the way to Him. Begin embracing YOUR crown today! Do you see it? Is the picture becoming clearer for you?

_____

_____

_____

_____

_____

_____

_____

_____

_____

_____

_____

_____

_____

_____

Pray. Seek. Listen.

Stay away from a fool, for you will not
find knowledge on their lips.
The wisdom of the prudent is to give thought to
their ways, but the folly of fools is deception.
Proverbs 14:7-9

Something we can truly appreciate and love about Jesus. He was savvy. Discerning. Well meaning. He wanted, and still wants, all of us to win. He forgives. He saves. He protects. He provides. He listens.

But watch this…while He was on this Earth, He confronted deception. He confronted the arrogant with their arrogance. He questioned the prideful regarding their pride, and He shot straight to the dark hearts of the religious Pharisees. In Matthew 23:13, the Lord said to them, "Woe to you, teachers of the law and Pharisees, you hypocrites! You shut the door of the kingdom of heaven in people's faces. You yourselves do not enter, nor will you let those enter who are trying to."

Jesus spoke TRUTH. He invited those that believed in Him to then follow Him. His every move was for His Father… our Father, with eternity ever on His mind. Your eternity and mine. Every word spoken from His lips embraced the entirety of humanity. Ultimately, He gave us the only answer we will ever need. Himself.

The statement below begs me to enter my prayer closet and ask God to show me much more wisdom in this area. May we be in the Word so we can KNOW the will of God, and the words of God. May we pray continually and ask Him to show us when to open a door, and when to shut it.

Do we continue to tolerate rude, hurtful, and harsh behavior? Or, once they clearly show us who they are, we should shake the dust off the bottoms of our feet and move on as scripture states in the New Testament.

Pray. Seek. Listen. Repeat. Answers WILL come.

♥ How does this devotion speak to you in your own circumstances?

_____

_____

_____

_____

_____

_____

_____

_____

_____

_____

_____

_____

His Peace

"Be anxious for nothing, but in everything by prayer and supplication with thanksgiving let your requests be made known to God. And the peace of God, which surpasses all comprehension, will guard your hearts and your minds in Christ Jesus."
Philippians 4:6-7

CHRISTOPHER SARDEGNA

I'm finding, the older I get, that trusting Him is getting easier. I don't have to stress over every detail. Why? First, because things have a way of working out. Secondly, and more importantly, is that He is omnipresent, omnipotent, and omniscient. How comforting that should be to us! If we trust Him…we won't be anxious. Anxiety is a fear of the future. The Holy Spirit revealed that to me many years ago. These things are ALL A PROCESS! Don't beat yourself up if you experience anxiety.

I encourage you to begin trusting Him. PRAY. Journal. Tell Him how you feel. Are you angry? Tell him. Write it out. Are you grateful? Share it. Are you believing for something? Trust Him with every detail. He cares deeply for every detail in your life. He wants you to experience His peace.

♥ Look up the definitions for omnipresent, omnipotent, and omniscient. How comforting it is to know that He is always, always here for you. He will never leave you.

_____

_____

_____

_____

_____

_____

_____

_____

_____

_____

_____

_____

Aspire to Inspire

It's not just about us, you know?
It's about leading others to freedom when
they're surrounded by darkness.
Caring for someone and expecting nothing in return.
Holding their hand and praying for
them when they feel all is lost.
Pointing them to hope. Helping them to breathe again.
There's a song…
♫ What the world needs now Is love, sweet love… ♫
Only LOVE from above can truly heal
us. Cleanse us. Forgive us.
Give us everlasting hope and joy.
May we aspire to inspire.

NATHAN LEMON

The Narrow Gate

Enter through the narrow gate. For wide is the gate
and broad and easy to travel is the path that
leads the way to destruction and eternal loss,
and there are many who enter through it.
Matthew 7:13

Life offers many paths. Some are born into wealth, power, and influence. Others simply are not. Those born into wealth, power, and influence may lead, but may struggle their whole lives with greed, addiction, control, pride, and even struggle having faith. Those born with less could also struggle. These people could carry heavy resentment and jealousy in their hearts. Always asking why they were cursed in this life.

It's interesting to think of which person would bend his knee first? The prideful rich person that is at the end of their rope, or the broke person that hates the whole world, including himself.

♥ Which one are you? Or are you somewhere in between just looking for direction? He wants you WHOLE, HEALED, and entering through the narrow gate.

_____

_____

_____

_____

_____

_____

_____

_____

_____

_____

_____

_____

_____

_____

_____

_____

_____

No Room

May the God of hope fill you with all joy and peace
as you trust in Him, so that you may overflow
with hope by the power of the Holy Spirit.
Romans 15:13

There is no room for selfishness. There is absolutely no room, or time, for jealousy. Quarrels must cease. Strife must end. Listen to the stirring of the Holy Ghost!

There is plenty of room for healing.

Let us make even more space to usher in the anointing of the Hoy Spirit.

Why, you ask? Because there are millions that need hope, healing, and salvation.

♥ If you are stuck in quarreling, jealousy, strife, or anything else that disrupts your peace, lay it down right here.

_____

_____

_____

_____

_____

_____

_____

Teach Our Children

If we confess our sins, he is faithful and
just and will forgive us our sins and
purify us from all unrighteousness.
1 John 1:9

When my children were young, I would place them in bed, and this is a scripture I taught them. It was the sweetest thing to hear their little voices recite these words. They are now grown. I sure miss those days.

We have such a tremendous responsibility and blessing to teach our children about Jesus.

♥ If you have children, I encourage you to teach them scripture. If you are praying to be a parent, TRUST Him with your situation.

_____

_____

_____

_____

_____

_____

_____

_____

Pure in Heart

Blessed are the pure in heart, for they will see God.
Matthew 5:8

PURE IN HEART = No ill motives. No selfish ambition. Choosing to live transparently. No deception. No coverups. A determination to be passionate about caring for others and having a heart that always wants the best for others. I choose THIS.

ARTEM BELIAKIN

Remember the truth that we are all in different seasons in life. Some are lost. Some are 'found', but still wandering in the desert. Some are growing in their faith. For all: Living water is right in front of us. Pouring out His Grace to each one of us…if we will JUST CHOOSE HIM.

As I was writing tonight, I looked up 'pure in heart'. An article I found by 'Got Questions Ministries' gave me some excellent additional insight: "Being pure in heart involves having a singleness of heart toward God. A pure heart has no hypocrisy, no guile, no hidden motives. The pure heart is marked by transparency and an uncompromising desire to please God in all things. It is more than an external purity of behavior; it is an internal purity of soul.

The only way we can be pure in heart is to give our lives to Jesus and ask Him to do the cleansing work. Psalm 51:10 says, "Create in me a pure heart, O God, and renew a steadfast spirit within me." God is the one who makes our hearts pure – by the sacrifice of His Son and through His sanctifying work in our lives (see also 1 John 3:1-3)." Choose HIM. It's so very simple.

The Good Stuff

Look to the Lord and his strength; seek his face aways.
I Chronicles 16:11

Trust Him.

Depend on Him.

Praise Him.

Talk to Him.

Find strength in Him.

Lean into Him.

♥ Write your very own short declaration of trusting Him below.

_____

_____

_____

_____

_____

_____

Live in Peace

Above all, love each other deeply, because love
covers over a multitude of sins.
I Peter 4:8

Don't live your life to make other people miserable. The
'make you pay because you did something that made me
unhappy' days need to GO! Everyone messes up at some point.
Everyone deserves some grace...including YOU! Now go patch
up your relationships and live in peace!

♥ Who do you need to make peace with? Ask God to show
you open doors for reconciliation. You will know when
the time is right.

_____

_____

_____

_____

_____

_____

_____

_____

_____

Grace...Beautiful Grace

However, I consider my life worth nothing to me; my
only aim is to finish the race and complete the task
the Lord Jesus has given me—the task of testifying
to the good news of God's grace.

Acts 20:24

GRACE. I woke up this morning to this one, beautiful
word. A new day to extend grace to myself and those around
me. It's easy to hold a grudge against someone, to determine to
not spend time with them, or some even choose to punish by
silence. Let's determine to extend grace today.

Here are some ways to begin:

- **START WITH YOU**. Yes. You deserve some grace, too.
- **JUST LET GO**. Quit carrying all that baggage around
  your shoulders.
- **LIVE IN GRATITUDE.** We have so much to be
  grateful for.
- **FORGIVE**. Forgive. Forgive.
- **APOLOGIZE WHERE NEEDED**. Don't hold onto
  your pride. Why do we even do that?
- **BE MINDFUL OF OTHERS**. It's not all about us.
  There's a whole world that needs grace extended.
- **SPEAK KINDLY**. Make every attempt to hold your
  tongue. The book of James has much knowledge related
  to this subject.

- **HAVE COMPASSION**. We all need this. Extend compassion. It's not that difficult to do.
- **ACCEPT PEOPLE FOR WHO THEY ARE**. This might be a tough one for many. We are all on a journey. Some are more enlightened than others. Some are not enlightened at all. Can we love them anyway...right where they are?

Extend grace today. Look in the mirror and start right there!

♥ **Write below the bullet points shown above (in bold letters). Personalize each point.**

_____

_____

_____

_____

_____

_____

_____

_____

_____

_____

_____

Expectations

For My thoughts are not your thoughts, nor are
your ways My ways," declares the Lord.
For as the heavens are higher than the earth,
so are My ways higher than your ways
And My thoughts than your thoughts.
Isaiah 55:8-9

LINA TROCHEZ

I've been doing a lot of reflection around the word EXPECTATIONS. Anytime we feel upset or angry, we might need to just take a step back. I have done this over the past few weeks. Let's consider if our expectations of something didn't happen the way we had hoped. We expect 'this' action OR we expect 'that' to work out a certain way. If then our expectations are not met it can cause feelings of upset, or even anger.

This is so simple. Join me in praying, "Lord God, I place my expectations into Your willing and capable Hands. Knowing that You care for me. That you are guiding me. And that, above all, You are gently guiding me down the right paths, even when I cannot see where it leads."

And remember...Abraham had no idea where he was going when he was sent...BUT he trusted God's Hand to place him at the right place. And certainly, at the right time.

♥ Do you get upset when your expectations are not met? How do you handle that situation?

_____

_____

_____

_____

_____

_____

_____

_____

_____

_____

_____

_____

_____

Pray

Pray for discernment. Even Jesus had a traitor in his circle of friends. One huge difference, when you have power from the Holy Spirit, is to NOT push them out of your life. Pray for them diligently. Pray that person will find their identity in Christ. Pray for their wounded heart to be healed and whole.

The Word says it's easy to love those that love us. Much harder to love those that don't. Luke 6:27-36 is a great read.

♥ Are there people in your life that are difficult to love?

_____

_____

_____

_____

_____

_____

_____

_____

_____

_____

Love Each Other

To love him with all your heart, with all your
understanding and with all your strength, and to
love your neighbor as yourself is more important
than all burnt offerings and sacrifices.
Mark 12:33

I will never, ever give up reaching out to others. We have
no idea if someone is about to give up. Allow compassion to
rise in your heart. Reach out beyond yourself to give hope to
someone that feels hopeless.

Don't hate anyone.

Don't wish to see someone fail.

Don't wish to see someone hurt.

Don't wish to see someone broken.

Don't wish to see someone face tragedy.

Just don't. Love each other.

♥ **How does this speak to you?**

_____

_____

_____

_____

_____

_____

True Purpose

For you created my inmost being; you knit
me together in my mother's womb.
I praise you because I am fearfully and wonderfully made;
your works are wonderful; I know that full well. My frame
was not hidden from you when I was made in the secret
place, when I was woven together in the depths of the earth.
Your eyes saw my unformed body; all the days ordained for
me were written in your book before one of them came to be.
How precious to me are your thoughts,[a] God!
How vast is the sum of them! Were I to count them,
they would outnumber the grains of sand –
when I awake, I am still with you.
Psalm 139:13-18

DANICA TANJUTCO

May we understand who we are, and why we were created:
in His image, for fellowship, to serve others, to be salt and light,
and to embrace that we are EXACTLY the way we were meant

to be. Once we understand our true purpose, there won't be time to dislike the person we see in the mirror.

♥ Who are you, friend? What do you feel your true purpose is?

_____

_____

_____

_____

_____

_____

_____

_____

_____

_____

_____

_____

_____

_____

Totally Transform

Jesus stopped and called them. "What do you want me to do for you? He asked. "Lord", they answered, "we want our sight" Jesus had compassion on them and touched their eyes. Immediately they received their sight and followed Him.
Matthew 20:32-34

NATHAN DUMLAO

These five powerful sentences say so much. "Lord, we want our sight."

Jesus knew what these men wanted before He even asked them. He wanted to hear their heart's desire. Two blind men, acknowledging His power by calling Him 'Lord', and then having the faith to ask for their sight.

Jesus was moved with compassion by their requests and their faith. He didn't ask what they could do for Him. He didn't require them to get their lives straightened out first. He didn't ask them what church they attended. He didn't ask them for anything. He simply touched their eyes. It changed them. These two men gained their eyesight that very day. They also gained spiritual eyes…and then chose to follow the very One that had the power to heal and save them from their former darkness.

Thank You, Father, for Your ability and desire to totally transform our lives from the inside out. Like a butterfly, you want to bring us out of our cocoon, and set us free.

♥ What do you want to ask God to do for you today?

_____

_____

_____

_____

_____

_____

_____

_____

_____

_____

_____

_____

An Orphan's Heart

If you love me, you will keep my commandments. And I will ask the Father, and he will give you another Helper, to be with you forever, even the Spirit of truth, whom the world cannot receive, because it neither sees him nor knows him. You know him, for he dwells with you and will be in you. "I will not leave you as orphans; I will come to you. Yet a little while and the world will see me no more, but you will see me. Because I live, you also will live...
John 14:15-21

BILL WEGENER

Do you have an orphan's heart? One that never feels at home. A heart that longs for a place of peace and belonging to call your very own? We do not have to live life out of an empty place within us. God is so willing to heal every hurt. Every wound. Every scar. Draw close to Him. He will never leave you. He will never turn you away.

♥ Let's talk about this. Have you felt you didn't belong?

_____

_____

_____

_____

_____

_____

_____

_____

_____

_____

_____

_____

_____

_____

_____

_____

_____

_____

_____

The Color of Our Skin

Love must be sincere. Hate what is evil; cling
to what is good. Be devoted to one another in
love. Honor one another above yourselves.
Romans 12:9-10

Let's shed a little light on the subject at hand. IF YOU SEE skin color before you see a human being with a heart, soul, and spirit...then may I suggest some time on your knees in prayer? Ask for hatred to be removed from your heart and replaced with compassion for other human beings.

REMEMBER and please never forget...we <u>all</u> bleed the same color.

ALEXANDER GREY

Remember My Chains

I, Paul, write this greeting in my own hand.
Remember my chains. Grace be with you.
Colossians 4:18

EYASU ETSUB

As I was reading tonight, this verse stood out to me. Paul, sitting in prison, writing to his friends in the church. In his own way...and in his own words, Paul asked for prayer by saying 'remember my chains'. The chains Paul spoke of were probably around his feet. In closing his letter, he wanted to ask his friends to not forget him. And to pray for him. The words He chose are very touching... 'remember my chains'.

What chains do you want to be removed in your life? Jesus can. Jesus will. Just ask. He's waiting to hear your voice.

♥ Where are you tonight in your heart, and in your head? What chains are around you?

_____

_____

_____

_____

_____

_____

_____

_____

_____

_____

_____

_____

_____

_____

_____

_____

_____

_____

The Journey

Be strong and courageous. Do not fear or be in
dread of them, for it is the LORD your God who goes
with you. He will not leave you or forsake you.
Deuteronomy 31:6

I so love the way God moves in our lives. The journey doesn't always make sense, but somehow, He works things out for our best and His glory. I believe my part in this journey, down all the pathways whether smooth or bumpy, is learning to trust His heart and listen for His voice and His gentle unwavering guidance and direction.

So grateful for a Heavenly Father that never forgets me nor abandons my heart.

♥ How is God moving in your life? What scriptures have spoken to your heart recently?

_____

_____

_____

_____

_____

_____

Choose Peace

Peace I leave with you; my peace I give to you. Not
as the world gives do I give to you. Let not your
hearts be troubled, neither let them be afraid.
John 14:27

TODAY your thoughts don't get to sabotage you! You know.... those thoughts that never end and keep you on a 'merry-go-round' of craziness. Listen to this! YOU can control your thoughts. YOU have been given a great mind! YOU have the power...take that power today! YOU determine where, when, and why these thoughts happen.

CHOOSE PEACE everyday...because it simply is yours for the taking.

♥ Do you have peace today? Write John 14:27 that is shown above, and then memorize.

_____

_____

_____

_____

_____

_____

_____

Location. Location. Location.

You will keep in perfect peace those whose minds
are steadfast because they trust in you.
Isaiah 26:3

YOUR REAL ESTATE TODAY IS... PEACE. When anything else presents itself ~ worry, fear, sickness, hopelessness ~ push those things aside and step into the power of the Holy Spirit.

God IS with us. Read His Word. Long to know Him. Seek healing. DESIRE to heal from your past. You NO LONGER LIVE THERE. Your real estate is right where you stand today... and YOU ARE WORTH IT.

FRANCESCA TOSOLINI

Broken Wings

Cast all your anxiety on Him because He cares for you.
I Peter 5:7

GASTON ROULSTONE

So many are going through heartbreak lately. Something has been on my mind lately...

We all experience broken wings. Those times that we simply cannot breathe deeply. Those moments when we would rather be swept away in slumber, and not think. When our thoughts are heavy like black, sticky tar. When our arms feel heavy. Remember...these moments do not last.

The sun will rise tomorrow. The moon will surely be in the sky. Your heart WILL feel lighter, though not today, it will sing again. Those moments of the light breeze blowing through your hair...when the birds are singing...and you awaken from your sorrowful sleep to a brighter, golden day.

Healing is coming. You will feel whole again. Your broken wings, love, will mend with time. Now sleep peacefully knowing there is a Heavenly Father above that is watching over you.

♥ Are your wings broken? Only He can mend you the way you need to be mended. Make this a prayer and ask to be whole and healed.

_____

_____

_____

_____

_____

_____

_____

_____

_____

_____

_____

_____

_____

_____

Season of Winter

Let us acknowledge the LORD; LET US press on
to acknowledge him. As surely as the sun rises,
he will appear; he will come to us like the winter
rains, like the spring rains that water the earth.
Hosea 6:3

Winter brings a chilling freeze right into our bones. Soft layers of snow fall and blanket the world as we know it. Underneath this

ALEX PADURARIU

snowy, white blanket are tender flowers being prepared to burst forth with new life…at just the right time. During winter, there are places of darkness, there is a stillness that lurks…making everything appear dormant, and lifeless, and lonely. Preparations have started. Spring will bring new growth and beginnings. One door closed…and a new door opened. New life will be experienced. And we will feel the warmth as the sunshine returns from its hidden place. The snow will begin to melt, as the warm sunshine touches all the frozen places. Melting away the cobwebs of darkness, the emptiness of the season, and welcoming us into this new space and new place. Exiting the former darkness, spring bursts forth! A new time to bloom, to feel whole, and a very special time for everything to be beautiful again. May we learn to find peace in winter knowing that spring is coming. A promise that it is never late…but right on time.

The Rest of the Story

GIORGIO PARRAVICI

Why do we learn more in the desert than on the mountain top? Let's consider Peter. Jesus clearly told Peter he would deny Him three times, but Peter could not even imagine denying his Lord. Test day came...and Peter failed miserably.

Imagine the moments and the days AFTER the denial. I've always envisioned this scene...Peter in a soggy, dreary alley surrounded and wrapped in cloaks of darkness...feeling completely devastated and destroyed inside. The dark valley he found himself in was one of carrying huge boulders of guilt on his shoulders. Certainly, this caused his head and heart to hang in complete shame and agony. The VERY ONE who loved him so dearly...he denied even knowing. Peter's value was depleted, and he was emptied of himself. BUT THE REST OF THE STORY GOES....Jesus restored Peter. One commentary stated "Jesus in restoring Peter to Himself removes any trace of self-righteousness within him. We will see how the Lord has to reveal to each disciple His sinfulness before he is ready to be effectively used and sent out by Him." A sobering statement. Out of darkness comes a bright light as Peter was completely restored by our Lord Jesus Christ. Soo after, Peter preached and led 3,000 to salvation in ONE day. Praise God! Our Lord. Our Healing God. Our Faithful Father.

Another great example. Elijah. In I Kings 19, we can follow a very interesting timeline as Elijah experiences a great victory only to find himself running for his life, falling beneath a tree, and stating to the Lord he was ready to just give up....and to NOW let him just die. Haven't some of us found ourselves in that darkness?

The Lord had a MUCH BETTER plan than Elijah did. The Lord sent provisions of food and water, through an angel of the Lord, for Elijah to eat and drink. He then instructed Elijah to get rest. AFTER Elijah did what the Lord told him to do (a lesson in itself), Elijah then traveled to Mount Horeb. Note the meaning of Horeb is "to be in ruins, lay in waste". The Lord asked him what he was doing. He stated that he had been zealous for the Lord and the others were not....DO YOU SEE IT? POSSIBLY Elijah was feeling like God had FORGOTTEN him in his well doing. He wanted to remind God where his heart was towards Him. Notice the Lord instructs Elijah to FIND HIM...The LORD said, "Go out and stand on the mountain in the presence of the LORD, for the LORD is about to pass by. Then a great and powerful wind tore the mountains apart and shattered the rocks before the LORD, but the LORD was not in the wind. After the wind there was an earthquake, but the LORD was not in the earthquake. After the earthquake came a fire, but the LORD was not in the fire. And after the fire came a gentle whisper. When Elijah heard it, he pulled his cloak over his face and went out and stood at the mouth of the cave." Elijah needed to find the Lord again. Think about it.... Elijah, a great prophet of God, ran away in fear when Jezebel threatened his life. Now God was instructing him to "GO OUT AND STAND".... Elijah was restored as the Lord gave him instructions on his next journey. Eventually Elijah was taken up into the clouds in a chariot. AMAZING!

Just a reminder that testing comes and we might fail miserably, but this prepares us for the next test. Failing only gives us even greater opportunity for future success. It's true.... disappointment may happen. Discouragement may fall.... BUT the REST OF THE STORY is there is always a new day, and restoration is just around the corner. Don't give up! His mercies are NEW every single morning. Place all your disappointments at the foot of the Cross. Lay your discouragement down. We don't have to carry it. We ALSO have a REST OF THE STORY, so be encouraged, and be listening for that still small voice to speak to your heart once again.

♥ How does this devotion speak to you regarding your own life?

_____

_____

_____

_____

_____

_____

The Heart's Choice

And do not grieve the Holy Spirit of God,
with whom you were sealed
for the day of redemption. Get rid of all
bitterness, rage, and anger, brawling
and slander, along with every form of malice. Be
kind and compassionate to one another, forgiving
each other, just as in Christ God forgave you.
Ephesians 4:30-32

LOUIS GALVEZ

Unforgiveness is the issue that my precious Savior has been 'whittling' away from the deepest chambers of my heart. I am learning, in this season of my life, that choosing to hold onto unforgiveness is nothing less than me deciding to be bitters towards those that have hurt me. We have all had, in the span of our lives, varying degrees of pain inflicted in some way that causes us to become overprotective of our heart. When we have been hurt, we build an invisible wall of protection around us to say, "I will never let anyone hurt me like that again." What we might not realize is that when we choose to say "never again" we are placing ourselves into a transparent prison that binds up the power God freely gives us to extend forgiveness to others.

Over the past several years, the Lord has continued to deal with me on this subject. He has lovingly drawn me to Matthew 18, and the deeply indebted servant. This servant was graciously extended forgiveness by his master only for that same forgiven servant to come against someone else that owed him a much smaller debt. How many times I have been guilty of being like that unforgiving servant with my own grip around someone's throat demanding immediate payment for my pain. According to the Word, this servant was handed over to be tortured until he paid back all that he owed. The servant's decision to hold onto his unforgiveness cost him dearly. We can read in Matthew 18:22 how Jesus said we are to forgive (get this) seventy TIMES seven. Does this mean that God does not allow us to fall short of what He requires? Is it possible that He allows us all times of adversity before we get to the other side of such sins as unforgiveness? I do believe He does allow us to "wallow" in the muck just as the prodigal son did. Remember that in the middle of the prodigal's "wallowing" it became very clear to him that something had to change, and that change had to begin with himself. Maybe THIS is the exact time that head knowledge finally becomes heart knowledge!

I'm so thankful that we serve a LOVING, VERY PATIENT Heavenly Father that desires His children to be healed, restored and whole!

Yes…God is giving me a clear vision of my Savior hanging painfully from the cross of Calvary as He prayed "Forgive them for they know not what they do." Can we SEE IT? God gave His perfect Heavenly example, through the gift of Jesus, of not only forgiveness but also meekness. Those unforgiving souls standing at the foot of the Cross were the epitome of ugliness as they spit their curses at WHO could be their life's greatest blessing.

Unforgiveness is ugly baggage to carry around for very long. It can cause our countenance to change and, without a doubt, completely steal our joy. Unforgiveness could also be compared to an emotional malignant cancer that feeds off the bitterness we clutch so tightly within us. The longer we choose to hold onto it the more miserable we are. Our Heavenly Father never created us to carry all these burdens we carry. He wants us to lean on Him, and to develop a deeper trust in Him so that we may know how to "cast our care on Him." (I Peter 5:7)

God's desire is for His children to repent, WITHOUT DELAY, when we feel the claws of bitterness taking root in our heart. What a revelation that we can choose to walk in His power and extend forgiveness to those that have wounded us.

Oh, Lord, may I never again make a choice to hold unforgiveness in my heart. Help me, Father, to always understand that You didn't have to forgive those at Calvary… You CHOSE to! In that same vein, if I make forgiveness a choice of my heart You will ALWAYS honor that choice. Yes…He freely gives us the power to extend forgiveness to others as forgiveness has been extended to us through His Son…and our Savior. How grateful we can be that God loves us too much to leave us where we.

♥ What bitterness do you hold in your heart? Are you ready to let it go?

_____

_____

_____

_____

_____

_____

_____

_____

_____

_____

_____

_____

_____

_____

_____

_____

Timing is Everything

5:00 AM and scripture swirls in my head. I've been meditating over these scriptures the past few days, and just how God has this beautiful, amazing way of speaking to us. He loves us when we're close, and He loves us when we're distant...going about the 'busy-ness' of our life.

Timing is everything, and He has made a special way to communicate with us through His word. How practical are these words in Ecclesiastes...and some of my very favorite words to cling to: "He has set eternity in the hearts of men."

No matter where we are today, we have a future to place in His very capable, loving Hands. No matter the hurt we have endured, we can be assured that he has a way to heal every wound. No matter the words that have caused pain, He has a way of breathing words of life into our spirit. With our successes, we can place them at the foot of the Cross and be ever so grateful for every blessing. His timing is perfect. His love is perfect. To know that He desires us to find satisfaction in our life...and what an incredible thought that you and I were created to fellowship with Him. His timing...our time. His master plan...our incredible future.

Love today.... live in it and every single moment life offers you today. Love, like Him, with an abandonment separating the layers of earthly influence, flesh, and dig deep into the very reason we're here.

Ecclesiastes 3: 1 – 8

There is a time for everything, and a season for every activity under heaven:

A time to be born and a time to die,
A time to plant and a time to uproot,
A time to kill and a time to heal,
a time to tear down and a time to build,
a time to weep and a time to laugh,
a time to mourn and a time to dance,
a time to scatter stones and a time to gather them,
a time to embrace and a time to refrain,
a time to search and a time to give up,
a time to keep and a time to throw away,
a time to tear and a time to mend,
a time to be silent and a time to speak,
a time to love and a time to hate,
a time for war and a time for peace.

Verse 11 and 12 says "He has made everything beautiful in its time. He has also set eternity in the hearts of men; yet they cannot fathom what God has done from beginning to end. I know that there is nothing better for men than to be happy and do good while they live. That everyone may eat and drink and find satisfaction in all His toil - THIS IS THE GIFT OF GOD. I know that everything God does will endure forever; nothing can be added to it, and nothing taken from it. God does it so that men will revere Him."

♥ Are you trusting His timing? Jot a prayer down below. Commit to trust Him!

_____

_____

_____

_____

_____

_____

_____

_____

_____

_____

_____

_____

_____

_____

_____

_____

_____

_____

To The Uttermost

Therefore, He is able also to save to the uttermost (completely, perfectly, finally, and for all time and eternity) those who come to God through Him, since He is always living to make petition to God *and* intercede with Him *and* intervene for them.
Hebrews 7:25

DENYS NEVOZHAI

Charles Spurgeon delivered his Sabbath evening message on June 8, 1856, on "Salvation to the Uttermost" with Hebrews 7:25 as his scripture base. In his words, "Nature is the spelling-book of man, in which he may learn his Maker's name, he hath studded it with embroidery, with gold, with gems. There are doctrines of truth in the mighty stars, and there are lessons written on the green earth and in the flowers upspringing from the sod. We read the books of God when we see the storm and tempest, for all things speak as God would have them; and if our ears are open, we may hear the voice of God in the rippling of the rill, in the roll of every thunder, in the brightness of every lightning, in the twinkling of every star, in the budding of every flower. God has written the great book of creation, to teach us what he is - how great, how mighty."

We are so unique. He made us that way. As he mentions, the rocks cannot experience salvation, nor the winds nor the waves or caves. We, however, were created with a little 'something something' special that is hollowed out with His name on it. That special hollowed, hallowed place called our spirit. That spirit, with bended knee and repentant heart, can be saved to the UTTERMOST. Completely. Perfectly. Finally....and for all time and eternity. What a promise! What comfort! We should never have a day that we feel we don't belong. We belong alright. He is our Father. We have His name written on our hearts and a place to call home. He has provided salvation to each one of us. He lovingly guides us, like a Master GPS, continually calculating and recalculating. Gently directing us towards a better, more fulfilling future. What a wonderful opportunity we've been given to be everything we can be while we're here.

Help us, God, to find complete fulfillment in You. Help us to find our purpose within Your will. And thank You, so much, for loving us the way You do. Let this life be more about You and less about us as You continually save us to the uttermost.

♥ Write your thoughts below.

_____

_____

_____

_____

For My Children

Love is the seed I'm planting
That unconditional kind
In my little children
In their sweet and precious minds
Filling their hearts with Jesus
And guiding them the way
That they should go...so they will know
His faithful love for them awaits.
Someday, when grown, if burdens seem
Much larger than their hopes and dreams
I pray that seed of love once placed
Will never question or erase
Their knowledge of their Heavenly Father
And of His love and saving grace.
And when I'm gone, I pray they'll be
Longing for eternity...
Both strong and wise in their Savior's ways
Knowing there's no other place
Like in the watch of their Shepherd's eyes
Filled with His tender mercy and grace
And love that they can always find...
Our Father's unconditional kind.

MARLENA COMPSTON

No Regrets

Forget the former things; do not dwell on the past. See, I am
doing a new thing! Now it springs up; do you not perceive it?
I am making a way in the wilderness
and streams in the wasteland.
Isaiah 43:18-19

My Mother used to say, "Today is the first day of the rest
of your life." She couldn't have been more right. Everyday
there is a beautiful beginning of our day as the sun rises...and
every evening there is an ending to it. The sun rises.... the sun
sets. The Word says in Lamentations that His mercies are new
every morning. Every single day we are presented with an
opportunity to make the very best of that day.

We all, no matter our age, can become so involved with
our own world and the 'busy-ness' of our world that we forget
to reach out to those we love. It's so easy to pick up the phone
and love on someone for a few minutes. A bouquet of flowers,
or homemade cookies, or a visit could mean the whole world
to someone.

I think of all the lonely people in the world that have no
one. Every single person needs to have a knowing that they
are special and that their lives matter. Just what's on my mind
tonight.

Lord God, help me to live with no regrets. To daily be
reminded of how terribly short life is, and that today is the first
day of the rest of my life. Help me to make it count....to bring
glory to You, Father, and to fulfill the calling You have placed
on my life. Forgive everything within me that has gotten ahead
of You and can tend to turn things upside down. I will always

be grateful that You are not the author of confusion. You bring great peace. You can be trusted from the beginning to the end. No regrets, Father, as I close my eyes to sleep tonight.

♥ Do you have regrets? Why not write each one on a piece of paper, and then either bury them in the ground or burn them in a fire pit? **TODAY** choose to let go of your regrets.

_____

_____

_____

_____

_____

_____

_____

ROYA ANN MILLER

An Ode of Love

In Memory of My Grandparents, W.S. and Iva Brown

Being family means more than we realize...
It means that we have a common bond between us
That getting along should be everything
That forgiving should be second nature
That peace should be sought at all costs
That hearts should be conquered
That love should grow stronger
As the years granted us go by.

Those precious people that brought us together
in this bond
Are now gone...but the same blood that flowed
through their veins
Proceeds, even now, through our own.
We are a family...the very by-products of two
hearts
Hearts interwoven in love more than eight decades ago.

MARLENA COMPSTON

Family means so much and it is so easy to forget...
How special each person is
How precious each moment should be
How short life is and how beautifully each family represents
The two people that began all this.

Grandma and Grandpa Brown, how we love you.
How we miss you....and still remember
The aroma of Grandma's cooking in the kitchen every morning at breakfast
Grandpa sitting on the porch in his rocking chair...his cane clutched
Between his worn, sunbaked hands,
Grandma as she carefully braided and wrapped her hair

Holding bobby-pins between her teeth...
The sound of the screen door slamming as grandkids ran in and out
The back porch where we all sat and ate watermelon and smelled the lilac bushes...
These memories we can only hold in our hearts
As we hold both of you now...
How we long to see you again.
How we want to be a family you'd be proud to call your own...
We are so very proud to be a part of you...
We lovingly remain your living legacies.

♥ I encourage you to write your own love letter or poem to your family. You can start right here...

_____

_____

_____

_____

_____

_____

_____

_____

_____

_____

Christmas Morning

ETIENNE DELORAINE

The wind blowing outside my window woke me up this early Christmas morning. Thank you, Father, for the sacrifice of your precious Son, sent in the form of a baby through a young girl that was willing to sacrifice everything for Your glory. As You always do, Lord God, in an amazing series of magical, supernatural events, You wrapped Jesus in swaddling clothes knowing all along His eventual steps towards the Cross…. the event that would reconcile us, Your beloved children, to You once again.

I've been pondering over the last week about fellowship and relationships. I recently had a house full of people that I love and care about. Fourteen beating hearts, happy smiles, loads of laughter…I couldn't have been happier. Last night was probably the first Christmas Eve I've ever spent *totally* alone. It made me keenly aware of the fact that I CAN be alone; however, there is nothing greater than being with those you love. This makes me think about the interesting possibility that God, in His 'incredibleness', before time even began was lonely for fellowship. You and I both know He doesn't 'need' us but what if... what if the Author of the universe decided to create us so that He could fellowship with us1 The Word speaks in Genesis of God walking in the garden to fellowship with Adam and Eve in the cool of the morning. My Grandmother used to sing the song "And He walks with me, and He talks with me, and He tells me that I am His own." The song is called "In the Garden".

So back to the thought of our Heavenly Father creating us, intricately molding us in our mother's womb, so that He could bring forth His own children to fellowship with. I so understand that this morning. Sitting on my couch, wrapped in my snuggle blanket that my son, Ross, gave me.

So here I sit. Snuggled near the Christmas lights softly twinkling in all their glory.... a keen knowing that what makes this woman truly content is being with those I love. Hearing their laughter...taking in every breath, and every moment knowing that moment never comes again. Father, it's so true that You're not in Heaven waiting for us to fail. You are waiting for that moment of glory when we lift our hearts to Heaven longing for time with You. You just want to be close to us and, as always, You are a wonderful, precious gentleman... never pushing Your will. Waiting, watching...just longing for moments of soft prayer to float to Heaven. I believe that You capture those beautiful, swirling sounds in Your Almighty arms and wrap them around You. Your Word says You even store our tears...what a beautiful thought!

This morning I thank You for Jesus. Thank You for the most glorious and thoughtful gift that could ever be given and placed on a tree in the form of a Cross. The gift of Your life laid down for those You love and long to spend all eternity with.

Outside my window this Christmas morning…lovely blankets and soft drifts of white snow wiping the slate of my entire world pure and beautiful for a new year to begin.

It's truly all about You, Jesus.

Samson and Delilah

Judges 13-16

Samson's calling was made known to his parents even before he was born. He was a promise to his parents, and they took great measures to follow God's instructions to rear him correctly. When he was young, he was loyal to God. As Samson grew up, he began to have an appetite for things outside of God's design for him. Does that sound familiar to anyone? Once grown, he manipulated his parents to marry a woman that he shouldn't have married. A marriage that had nothing but heartbreak for him. Then out of anger and great disappointment, he fell in love with Delilah and ushered a very deceptive, scheming, and dark force into his life. His lust for her and his determination to win her love proved nothing but emptiness for him. Sadly, Samson compromised the beautiful gift that had been given to him before birth.... a tremendous calling to free God's people. His disobedience and irresponsibility cost him so much.

When we look at Delilah and her motives, we see that she had a very selfish agenda with Samson. She wanted to bring Samson down...all the while lining her pockets with silver willingly paid to her by the Philistines. Samson's agenda was to ultimately have love and happiness but they both escaped him. Delilah, it appears, was sent into his life to destroy his confidence, steal his joy, thwart the call on his life and set him up for complete failure. She clung to him like a bad grape on a green vine. As powerful as Samson was, and as anointed as his life had been, he just could never prune Delilah from his life.

We must remember that Samson was as human as we are. If only.... he had focused on the call on his life. If only...he had bent his knee and heart totally to God and waited on God's timing. Instead, he was continually sought after by his Philistine enemies. He was betrayed by the woman he desired to share his life with, he chose to compromise the calling on his life and, devastatingly, lost his life.

In looking over the entire story of Samson, the truths that I see are:

- In his anger and disappointment, Samson's FAITH DECREASED
- In his desire to fulfill his life outside of God, Samson LOST his FOCUS
- As he continued in his disobedience, Samson's POWER was COMPROMISED
- Ultimately, Samson's LIFE was EXTINGUISHED

May we never allow ANYTHING or ANYONE to pull us down into an abyss that causes us to lose ourselves. May we never lose our focus. May we never be willing to give up our dreams or our calling and purpose. May we choose to be OVERCOMERS and NEVER be overcome...except by our Savior...who ALWAYS causes us to be powerful and confident in Him.

In closing, I choose to follow Him and fulfill the call on my life. My favorite scripture in Psalms 37:4 says, "Delight yourself in the Lord and He will give you the desires of your heart." May our hearts be divinely focused. May our desire be to love Him. May our lives have not EVEN a hint of disobedience, but of confidence in who we are in Him.

♥ How does this devotion speak to your heart? Do you have times you say, 'if only'? God can redeem ALL your regrets.

_____

_____

_____

_____

_____

_____

_____

_____

_____

_____

_____

_____

_____

_____

_____

_____

More than A Conqueor

In his book "My Utmost for His Highest", Oswald Chambers said, "Our yesterdays present irreparable things to us; it is true that we have lost opportunities which will never return, but God can transform this destructive anxiety into a constructive thoughtfulness for the future. Let the past sleep but let it sleep on the bosom of Christ. Leave the irreparable past in His hands and step out into the irresistible future with Him."

Father God, You are the lover of my soul, my gatekeeper, the One who sees what my life is all about. I praise You for making me more than a conqueror, an overcomer, a visionary, a listener of Your voice, a seeker of Your will – You, Father, are truly awesome! Help me, dear Lord, to raise my head up and walk boldly and gracefully through this life.... full of grace, unwavering and with a spirit of love even when it's the most difficult. Father, I ask for simplicity, consistency, commitment, assurance, holiness, trust, restoration, authority, submission, and clarity. You never leave us.... you never forsake us. I am so very grateful for Who You are and for the promise of a great and wonderful future. Amen.

♥ Write your own prayer below. Oswald also said, "Prayer does not equip us for greater works— prayer is the greater work."

_____

_____

_____

_____

Distractions

Seek first the kingdom of God and His righteousness
and all these things shall be added to you.
Matthew 6:33

The Lord is so faithful. As I was laying on the couch last night, wrapped up in a blanket and not feeling well AT ALL, my thoughts were on how distracting the world can be. Think of just how MANY thoughts go through our head in just one day!

The Word says to "take every thought captive". Just part of what we might go through in one morning.... the alarm goes off, we're out of bed, and then thoughts begin 'streaming' through our mind. The Word speaks of Jesus starting His day in the early morning. Mark 1:35 says "And rising very early in the morning, while it was still dark, he departed and went out to a desolate place, and there he prayed." The Lord knew He needed a 'game plan' for the day, and He wanted to spend time with His Father.

I must admit I am SO much more a 'night' person than a 'morning' person. I get drops into my spirit more in the late-night hours or while I'm driving. This is just what works for me, but what a better plan it could be to get up early and seek Him first... before the day truly begins! Maybe then all the crazy thoughts that can drift through our minds can be spiritually filtered FIRST before they start. Some thoughts that come through our heads..... hope the traffic's not bad....what to wear.....is it cold outside?.... what about that meeting today?....oh my....I wish I hadn't said that yesterday...what if I lost my health, job, spouse, friends, etc...what if...what if...what if.....see where our heads can take us? So simple.

Let's make a choice to seek Him early, seek His design and desire for the day, and then place all our cares and concerns at the foot of the loving Cross and just walk away.

Distractions don't have to rule us. Distractions don't have to define us. Father God, help us to take 'every single thought captive'. What does that really mean? It means to discipline your mind to not let it be placed on a merry-go-round that never stops. YOU determine what comes through your thoughts. You don't entertain every random thought that hits your mind. Take hold of a foundation within your thoughts and stand firmly in what you truly know.... which leads me to share Philippians 4:8, 9 "Finally, brothers, whatever is true, whatever is noble, whatever is right, whatever is pure, whatever is lovely, whatever is admirable - if anything is excellent or praiseworthy - think about such things. Whatever you have learned or received or heard from me or seen in me - put it into practice. And the PEACE OF GOD will be with you."

♥ What are your distractions? When do you spend your quiet time with Him? Seek first His kingdom...and all these things will be added to you: peace, joy, provision, hope and more!

_____

_____

_____

_____

_____

_____

Make A Difference

Do not conform to the pattern of this world but be transformed by the renewing of your mind. Then you will be able to test and approve what God's will is—his good, pleasing and perfect will.
Romans 12:2

Simple question. Aren't we all broken? Pretty much. As we begin to heal, and continue to heal, let us choose to make a difference in this life. So, basically, we can 'look out for number 1' by acknowledging who IS 'number one'. And... come to terms that it's not us!

The Word says to be salt and light. To choose life. To cling to Him. To not conform to this world but be transformed.

IAN STAUFFER

How? By renewing our mind, being in the Word, allowing the Holy Spirit to mold us and grow us. He certainly will be faithful to do exactly that. Side note...in His time, and not ours.

I promise...it is so rewarding to share the Lord Jesus Christ and explain their very own personalized gift of salvation. Especially when they feel hopeless, and you stand in awe watching Him navigate futures and transform lives. I promise He is a faithful character builder, a confidence instiller, has the nurturing heart of a mother, and is most certainly a compassionate and caring Father.

♥ Where do you need to stop conforming to this world? What do you need to lay down, and choose to be salt and light instead?

_____

_____

_____

_____

_____

_____

_____

_____

_____

_____

_____

_____

_____

_____

_____

_____

_____

Beautiful Pages

JANKO FERLIC

BOOKS. I LOVE BOOKS. I mean I R-E-A-L-L-Y love books. I have books ranging from J. Oswald Sanders "Spiritual Leadership" to Southern Living cookbooks. Yes…I read cookbooks, too.

I have my very favorite books like "The Confident Woman" by Ingrid Trobisch. Ingrid, a beautiful-spirited former missionary who was married to missionary Walter Trobisch. The name of Ingrid's home was "Haus Geborgenheit" which is German for "a place of steadfast shelter". Isn't that beautiful? She tells the story of one of her mother's last Christmas letters stating, "My hands tremble, my legs are unsteady, but my heart is strong and my love for you is unchanging." THAT statement alone could change many a heart that feels alone in the world.

The great thing about a wonderful book is this... I can FEEL it in my hands. Not only can I feel the bound book in my hands, but I can take my pen and prayer journal all OVER it if I want to, and believe me, I DO! I can underline precious words of wisdom. I can date my journal entries and then...years later...take the book off its shelf, dust it off and just like a faithful friend treasure the book like brand new.... reading the words that I journaled in years gone by. Filling my heart, once again, with the book's knowledge.

I just pulled out a few of my favorite books tonight and read through some of the entries that I'd like to share with you. I don't mind opening my journals to you because it is part of the call on my life. To expose my heart might help point you to His heart....to be real with you might hit something in you that will cause you to launch out and reach for your FULL potential!

A journal entry I dated October 23, 1999, in a book by the anointed Beth Moore... "A Heart Like His" – "Heavenly Father, As I begin this journey this night, I simply must lift my heart, my hands and the Spirit within me to You! YOU ARE WORTHY OF PRAISE! You are Holy, O Lord Most High! Thank You for being the jealous God You are! For pursuing me without ever abandoning me – for loving me without ever pushing me away – for seeing through all my insecurities, the inabilities and the girl's heart within me. For I truly know that You love me with an everlasting love!"

THOSE words are so meaningful to me and gives me such a glimpse as to exactly where I was late one night in 1999. In my very FIRST Bible that my parents gave me on December 25, 1971, I wrote the words of my former Pastor Andrew O'Kelley, "Expect Jesus any minute, but live like it will be 100 years!"

While teaching a women's Bible study, I penned a quote found in the book "Captivating" by Stasi and John Eldredge:

"Your heart as a woman is the most important thing about you."
Just beautiful.

Lastly, I'll share what I wrote in my Executive EQ book while in Chicago one winter. It was 11:00 PM on Friday, December 3rd and snowing was gently falling outside. I was alone in the restaurant on the first floor at the Drake Hotel. A piano was being played softly in the background, and there was low hustle and bustle all around me. I had myself pulled into my own 'reading world'. I can remember the smell in the air as I took my pen and wrote "What an amazing journey 2010 has been! 2011 will prove to be even more exciting and so many dynamics of life to discover! I can't WAIT to see what all God has in store!"

In closing, books have the most beautiful pages placed between the front and the back covers and, most importantly for me, part of my life lovingly tucked between the pages with my written prayers and journaling.

♥ Are you also a reader? Do you journal in your books? What is your favorite book or author?

_____

_____

_____

_____

_____

_____

_____

Surrender

Love the Lord your God with all your heart,
and with all your soul, and with all your
strength, and with all your mind; and
love your neighbor as yourself.
Luke 10:27

JON TYSON

We say "God, you can have everything in my life BUT PLEASE....not that one small area.... that one small chamber in my heart. No. Not that. OHHHH! But He is FAITHFUL to want the diamond that is buried in the darkest chambers of your heart. He isn't nearly as interested in the small stones that are easy for you to give up.... those that are superficially laying in the first couple of layers within your heart. He wants the perfect diamond that must be carefully and patiently excavated for THIS is what holds the key to your deepest fears and your GREATEST FREEDOM. He wants the key to unlock those doors to unleash joy and strength in your heart.

REMEMBER that He is a gentleman and will never force His way. He is waiting for you to ask Him in. Let me encourage you to lay your face before Him. Surrender that which is buried. Allow Him to resurrect the death inside your heart to release an amazing GUST of new life from within you.

Breathe IN forgiveness.... EXHALE bitterness.

Breathe IN laughter...EXHALE sorrow.

Breathe IN light-heartedness.... EXHALE heaviness.

Embrace a new beginning and LET GO of the old, dead, rotting bones knowing FULLY that HE is the power, the resurrection, and the life...the LIFE GIVER.

Choose THIS day, the Word states, whom you will serve. Are you just dead, dry bones with hidden, buried diamonds or a POWERFUL man or woman of God that can STRETCH YOUR ARMS before Heaven and say "OH GOD...use me for Your purposes.... for YOUR glory. You can have access to every place., Lord. Every chamber is yours."

This is the cry of my heart for you. This is the prayer within me for your complete and total healing. YOU are why I wrote this book.

♥ Surrender to Him. It will be THE BEST DECISION you have ever made in your life.

_____

_____

_____

_____

_____

Brought to My Knees

Oh come, let us worship and bow down; Let us kneel
before the Lord our Maker. For He is our God, and we
are the people of His pasture, and the sheep of His hand.
Psalm 95:6,7

I heard a song on Thursday night called "Brought to My
Knees". You know me.... driving home I started pondering
the significance of kneeling in prayer. During my search
this morning, I found several thoughts on this. One thought
being that 'kneeling is the ultimate posture of submission and
surrender. To kneel is to indicate, by bodily attitude, a total
submission of our minds and hearts to the true Presence of
Christ.' Another commentary stated that "We throw ourselves
down and so acknowledge where we are and who we are:
fallen creatures whom only He can set on their feet. We throw
ourselves down, as Jesus did, before the mystery of God's power
present to us, knowing that the Cross is the true burning bush,
the place of the flame of God's love, which burns but does not
destroy."

In Acts 7:59,60 "And they stoned Stephen as he was calling
on God and saying "Lord Jesus, receive my spirit," then he knelt
and cried out with a loud voice, "Lord do not charge them with
this sin." That brings tears to my eyes. Stephen, in the very last
moments of his life, certainly in distress and much pain, fell to
his knees before God in total submission. He was completely
innocent of any charges yet, just as our Lord Jesus on the Cross,
cried out for God to not hold charge against the very ones that
were taking his life.

In Mark 14:33-36, we read the account where Jesus was in a very stressful time right before He was given over to be crucified; very troubled, deeply distressed, and sorrowful.... falling on the ground in prayer to pour His heart out before His Heavenly Father. 'And He took Peter, James, and John with Him, and He began to be troubled and deeply distressed. Then He said to them, my soul is exceedingly sorrowful, even to death. Stay here and watch. He went a little farther, and fell on the ground, and prayed that if it were possible, the hour might pass from Him. And He said "Abba, Father, all things are possible for You. Take this cup away from Me; nevertheless, not what I will, but what You will.' The humility you hear in His prayer...the choice He made to be completely emptied of Himself and on His knees crying out to God for help through these very dark moments of anxiety.

In my scripture search this morning, I found a journal entry I wrote in my Max Lucado Inspirational Study Bible dated December 10, 1997:

My Bible sits there faithfully

Full of wisdom, full of prayers

All the answers that I need

With head bowed and bended knee.

Lord, help me seek You everyday

Help me love in every way

To mirror Your life, Your special grace

Help me always seek your face.

I leave you with the thought to find a quiet place today and bend your knee to Him in worship and adoration. Pour out your heart before Him and listen as He pours out His heart towards you.

Homeless Heart

For I know the plans I have for you, plans to not
harm you but to give you hope and a future.
Jeremiah 29:11

JOHN MOESES BAUAN

I was driving east on the highway. Like a quick flash, I passed a homeless man that was picking up cans on the side of the highway. My heart went out to him, and I lifted him up in prayer asking the Lord about him. At 65 mph, I didn't see him but for a very brief second. What I did catch was his tattered clothing, a weathered profile, and a stocking cap on top of his long, scraggly, silver hair. Please, Lord, bless him. Miles down the road, I couldn't help but think about what happened in his life to find himself where he was. Maybe he lost his family? His home? His ability to support himself?

The message that came to me was wondering where YOU are today. Do you need a home for your heart? Have you found yourself feeling bankrupt in life and wondering if things will ever get better? Did you lose your way somewhere along the road of life? Take a wrong turn or lose your directions? Maybe someone left you on the side of the road, alone and sitting with an empty tank. Are you picking up trash along the side of highways named depression, discouragement or unforgiveness?

According to scripture in Ephesians, we have been given a GLORIOUS INHERITANCE! God never created you with any intention of dropping you on the side of a desolate highway.... all alone and without purpose. He has promises all throughout the Word that you can get in your head and your heart to better understand what your life is about.

One of my favorite scriptures is Jeremiah 29:11, "For I know the plans I have for you, plans to not harm you but to give you HOPE AND A FUTURE." There have been times in my life I held on to that scripture like it was my *very breath*. I encourage you to read that every single day until you have that knowledge from your head to your heart and from your heart to your head. Write it down and place it in front of you. Determine your heart will *no longer* remain without a home. Take yourself off the side of the highway today.

Get back on the road to finding your place in this world. Get in the Word, which is your map, and you will find the directions to everything you need. It will be so worth the journey!

♥ Does your heart have a home? Declare today to place your faith in Him every single day.

_____

_____

_____

Focus then Trust

Wait for the Lord; be strong, and let your heart
take courage, yea, wait for the Lord!
Psalm 27:14

Question posed. Where's your focus? It's so easy to get our focus on other things besides what we should be focusing on.... or should I say.... WHO we should be focusing on. I, for one, am guilty.

I talked with a very dear friend today that recently ended a relationship. Immediately their thoughts were to get on a dating website and start looking for love again. My advice to my friend today was: 1) give yourself time to heal, 2) don't buy into the world's way of finding the right one and, most importantly, 3) PLEASE allow God time to bring the right person into their life. Disclaimer: I DO know several couples that have met through a dating site so don't think it 'can't ever happen'. Just be very cautious, as there are many lost souls just looking for a place to land.

Here's the truth. His plan is perfect. His timing is perfect. My concern, for my friend, is that they will go right back into the cycle of dating, get caught up in the whole thing again and then be right back in a 'wrong' relationship again wasting precious time.

GOD wants us to FOCUS on Him and, even better, to TRUST Him completely! That's something I have had to deal with this past year.... have I TRUSTED HIM? I'm sure I've written about it before...I trust Him with my salvation (that He so lovingly imparts), I trust Him with the care of my children (that He so graciously shares) BUT I was not trusting Him with other important issues in my life.

There's SO much more to life than us choosing to go down the wrong path. It's so very simple to make those paths straight. Start by TRUSTING Him. TRUST Him. TRUST Him! What truly do you have to LOSE?

Did you know the definition for trust is 'assured reliance on the character, ability, strength, or truth of someone or something'. Lord, help us to get that from our head to our heart and then also from our heart to our head. Please read it again with the focus around trusting God....ASSURED RELIANCE on the character, ability and strength of a Heavenly Father that has such a glorious, great promise of a future for each one of us! You see.... HIS plan for us is so much more creative and colorful and exciting than we could possibly dream up ourselves! And, best of all, He sees us through the blood of Jesus....completely redeemed.

Yes, it's true, we mess up, BUT that is what it's all about. He continues to stretch out His arms to us.... JUST like the Faithful Heavenly Father He is.... never letting go. He always focuses on us, believes in us and is always on our side.

♥ Write the definition of trust below. Know that He has a great plan for you. Begin trusting Him with all the details of your life.

_____

_____

_____

_____

Just As I Am

Expectations. Offenses. Criticisms. Judgements. We can place so much weight on others and even ourselves. Remember that old hymn "Just as I Am"? It was written in 1836 by a woman named Charlotte Elliott. Interesting story. Charlotte was presented the gospel by a man she met and was quite offended by his presentation of the gospel to her. Weeks later, she confessed she was earnestly seeking her Savior and asked the same man, César Malanto who had previously offended her, to lead the way for her to know her Savior.

I've taken the liberty of placing a more modern twist to two of the stanzas in her famous hymnal:

> Just as I am, though tossed about
> With many a conflict, many a doubt
> Fightings and fears within without
> O Lamb of God, I come, I come.
> Just as I am, poor, wretched, blind;
> Sight, riches, healing of the mind,
> Yes, all I need is You to find
> O Lamb of God, I come, I come.

Are there criticisms all around you because you don't fit someone else's mold of who you are supposed to be? Expectations laid out by others of what you're supposed to look like. Act like? Dress like? KNOW THIS! You are precious just as you are. His Word says that He's changing us from "glory to glory". Every day we live....and breathe....and learn....and see. Yes....we may fall but only to wake up the next morning with a clean slate and a new day!

If anyone has spoken against you, or if you have placed far too much pressure on your own shoulders.... then LAY IT DOWN and stretch your arms to the Heavens. Breathe IN.... breathe OUT and say, "I am loved JUST AS I AM". It's truly that simple. Get it from your head to your heart....and then your heart to your head.

♥ Say it out loud "I am loved JUST AS I AM." He loves you with every drop of blood that He shed on the Cross. AND...He would have done the same thing if it were ONLY YOU.

_____

_____

_____

_____

_____

_____

_____

LORENZO SPOLETI

Broken Hearts Can Be Mended

Jesus said, "Father, forgive them, for they
do not know what they are doing.
Luke 23:24

A friend told me this past week that due to her husband cheating on her she thought she could never trust again. (Shared with permission.) I have meditated on these comments all week and prayed over them to receive some revelation on these feelings of devastation and hurt. I had a few things come to my heart that I want to share with you. This is written to give you hope if you have found yourself in this situation.

First, I believe that the person that cheated didn't do it to hurt you. People that cheat do this because there is (or was) a huge hole in their heart that only God can fill. They are unhappy and always seeking something or someone to make them happy. You could have done everything in life perfectly with a capital "P" and still found yourself in the relationship with this person. They have huge gaping wounds that need to be healed. The ONLY ONE that can heal them is Jesus.

Let's visit the Garden of Eden where Adam and Eve lived in a pure and perfect world. Even though life was great they still chose to break God's trust and covenant. They decided to 'cheat' on God believing the grass was greener on the other side. Their decision hurt the heart of God deeply. It certainly did not catch Him by surprise, but their choice was to sever the wonderful relationship they enjoyed with God. The closeness was gone. The deep intimacy and walks in the Garden were history. As we all know, there were deep reaching consequences for their actions that we still suffer today. BUT SEE THIS....God had a plan!

The garments the Lord God made for Adam and Eve didn't come free.... a spotless lamb was sacrificed to cover their sin. Much later, another Lamb was sacrificed. As the Lamb of God hung on the Cross, many stood below him hurling insults and throwing their anger and bitterness towards Him.

Notice THIS! He didn't rebuke them! He didn't respond to their painful insults, hurled fists and cutting words. He turned His bleeding head towards Heaven and prayed to the Father FOR them. Luke 23:34 "Jesus said, "Father, forgive them, for they do not know what they are doing." What an amazing statement of love and humility. His ego was not in the way, He wasn't demanding His rights, He simply prayed for those who so deeply hurt Him. They didn't take His life. He willingly laid it down for all of us.

The truth is this.... people hurt us. Some mean to...some do not. Some just truly don't know any better because they are so wounded themselves. God never intended for you to go through the hurts you have endured. The GOOD NEWS is that we can have kingdom living right here within our own hearts. He is our Protector and our Shield. Jesus chose.... though giving His ALL for us.... He chose forgiveness and understood that those that hurt Him truly didn't understand the fullness of their actions. Should we forgive? Yes. Do we forget? That will be between you, the circumstance, and our Heavenly Father. The best part is your past hurts don't equal your future. There is a beautiful, golden plan for you. Step into it today and humble yourself before God. I encourage you to write down the name(s) of those that have hurt you, cheated on you, deserted you. Once they are written, ask God to help you to forgive every single name. Then tear up this piece of paper and toss it in the trash. Choose freedom from any scars that were placed on your heart! Today is your day of freedom!!!

♥ Here's the beginning of your list. Use separate pages if you need to. It's time to forgive those that have hurt you, cheated on you, lied about you, and devastated you. Simply write their name. God knows the situation(s). TODAY is a great day to place it under the blood and begin to forgive. The Holy Spirit gives us the power to do exactly that... FORGIVE.

_____

_____

_____

_____

_____

_____

_____

_____

_____

_____

_____

_____

_____

_____

Amazing Words

DIANA SIMUMPANDE

Galatians 5:13-26 says "You, my brothers and sisters, were called to be free. But do not use your freedom to indulge the flesh; rather, serve one another humbly in love. For the entire law is fulfilled in keeping this one command: "Love your neighbor as yourself." If you bite and devour each other, watch out or you will be destroyed by each other. So I say, walk by the Spirit, and you will not gratify the desires of the flesh. For the flesh desires what is contrary to the Spirit, and the Spirit what is contrary to the flesh. They conflict with each other, so that you are not to do whatever you want. But if you are led by the Spirit, you are not under the law. The acts of the flesh are obvious: sexual immorality, impurity, and debauchery; idolatry and witchcraft; hatred, discord, jealousy, fits of rage, selfish ambition, dissensions, factions, and envy; drunkenness, orgies, and the like. I warn you, as I did before, that those who live like this will not inherit the kingdom of God. But the fruit of the Spirit is love, joy, peace, forbearance, kindness, goodness, faithfulness, gentleness, and self-control. Against such things there is no law. Those who belong to Christ Jesus have crucified the flesh with its passions and desires. Since we live by the Spirit, let us keep in step with the Spirit. Let us not become conceited, provoking, and envying each other."

So much wisdom and truth. Wrap your head and heart around each one. Meditate on them. Allow the Holy Spirit to teach you. If you have not taken that step quite yet, TODAY can be YOUR day of salvation.

♥ IS your heart where it needs to be? Where are you struggling today? PRAY for peace. Ask God to continue healing you through and through. Be prepared ~ He will!

_____

_____

_____

_____

_____

_____

_____

_____

_____

Know Your Tribe

"I alone cannot change the world, but I can cast a stone across the water to create many ripples."
Mother Teresa

Remember that as we step into each new day, not everyone will be on our same page. Not everyone will believe in what we do or want to be a part...BUT REMEMBER...there are those that will embrace us. THEY will welcome the gifts, talents, and skills we bring. THEY will need what we have. THOSE are the ones we are called to. THOSE are our tribe.

♥ Do you know who your support system is?

_____

_____

_____

_____

_____

_____

_____

_____

_____

God Knows

For I know the plans I have for you, declares
the Lord, plans to prosper you and
not to harm you, plans to give you hope and a future.
Jeremiah 29:11

Anger can certainly disguise itself. Many people are just bottom line angry with God. We can get stuck in the grieving process: denial, anger, bitterness, and grief are a few to mention. Maybe our circumstances aren't what we had hoped. Or we've experienced loss. We might be feeling forgotten, broken, left out, or abandoned.

God knows. Share it with Him. I encourage you to pray. Ask the Lord to reveal any anger that is stored within you. Then begin sifting through it, all the while praying, until nothing is left but ashes that can be blown away with one strong breath.

♥ Share your thoughts after reading this. Pray and expose the anger within. It is SO worth it. Begin dealing with it this very day.

_____

_____

_____

_____

_____

_____

His Spoken Words

Driving to work this morning I was thinking about just how faithful God is. He is true to His word. I was remembering many words He's spoken personally to my heart over the last ten years...

"It is well with my soul." His message to me during a troubled time. Words to remind me that HE is in control and guiding my journey. It's MY lesson to learn to trust Him. It's easy to trust Him with our salvation...that seems a given. It's not difficult to trust Him with my children and their lives, HOWEVER, there is an area or two in my life that I realize I don't give Him full access. His words...simply put...."Marlena, let it be well with your soul and trust me!"

"I am under no obligation to bless you when you choose to step into something I didn't first begin". Hard lesson when we follow something God is saying no to.

"I am longsuffering, but I have a limit." Only a loving Father would speak these words. When we're off too far to the right or the left...He will lovingly guide us back to center. That's a promise!

"Don't fight for I will take care of you." And after nine years of being on my own again, He has proven Himself faithful to these words spoken to me in 2001.

"If I have to make you a fool to make you wise, I will do so." Tough lesson many years ago and a true and good lesson in discernment of those that care about you and those that don't. No matter the situation or relationship realize that everyone won't be your best friend. Learn to lean on God and not on people. He's our acceptance and He's more than enough.

"Let go"." Hard words to receive when you don't want to hear those words. Have you ever asked God for answer to a prayer and then HE ANSWERED, and the answer was far different than what you had planned or hoped for? HE KNOWS what is best! He knows the plans He has for us.... therefore, best to listen and 'let go'.

I'm learning, more and more, to be obedient to His Word and to His words spoken to me personally. Something I heard last week was "Slow obedience is no obedience." Let us be "immediately" obedient once He pierces our heart with truth. Our best is what is at the center of our Father's heart. We can trust that and never doubt it. We are dearly loved and given the gift of eternity.

♥ What is God speaking to your heart today?

_____

_____

_____

_____

_____

_____

_____

_____

_____

The Full Armor of God

An incredible passage to put to memory is Ephesians 6:10-20: "Finally, be strong in the Lord and in his mighty power. Put on the full armor of God, so that you can take your stand against the devil's schemes. For our struggle is not against flesh and blood, but against the rulers, against the authorities, against the powers of this dark world and against the spiritual forces of evil in the heavenly realms. Therefore, put on the full armor of

MARIO LA PERGOLA

God, so that when the day of evil comes, you may be able to stand your ground, and after you have done everything, to stand. Stand firm then, with the belt of truth buckled around your waist, with the breastplate of righteousness in place, and with your feet fitted with the readiness that comes from the gospel of peace. In addition to all this, take up the shield of faith, with which you can extinguish all the flaming arrows of the evil one. Take the helmet of salvation and the sword of the Spirit, which is the word of God. And pray in the Spirit on all occasions with all kinds of prayers and requests. Be alert and always keep on praying for all the Lord's people. Pray also for me, that whenever I speak, words may be given me so that I will fearlessly make known the mystery of the gospel, for which I am an ambassador in chains. Pray that I may declare it fearlessly, as I should."

Put your armor on every day. Be well equipped and prepared.

Clarity of A Diamond

I delight greatly in the LORD; my soul rejoices in
my God. For he has clothed me with garments of
salvation and arrayed me in a robe of his righteousness,
as a bridegroom adorns his head like a priest, and
as a bride adorns herself with her jewels.
Isaiah 61:10

BAS VAN DEN EIJKHOF

The diamond is the most precious of all stones. It is white
in color and beautifully transparent. As I googled to find out
more, I learned that diamond clarity describes either the absence
or presence of flaws inside or on the surface of a diamond. A
perfect stone with perfect clarity or clearness is rare, and most
flaws that do exist cannot be seen without looking at it through
a jeweler's magnifying glass. 'Oh Lord! May our hearts be
beautifully transparent before You! May our hearts be lovingly
transparent towards those around us. May we be REAL and not
a false version but what You desire for us to be.... genuine." The

scripture in Isaiah speaks of our soul rejoicing in Him…. and….
amazing that He clothes us with garments of salvation and
then arrays us in a robe of His righteousness. Notice these are
things HE takes care of…. we just must have a willing heart and
one that delights and rejoices in Him. "Lord, help us to have
clarity as a flawless diamond, though knowing we will never be
completely perfect while in this world, we can certainly trust
You to polish and refine us as You move us towards the plan
You have purposed for our lives."

A Glimpse of Paradise and Poverty

Arriving in Cozumel, I loaded my things into the tiny rental car, a Dodge Attitude, and took off into the streets of Cozumel. Windows down…and the back streets were filled with happy, Spanish-speaking voices, and festive music blaring from the radio. I zipped around the streets like I owned the place! It didn't take me long to figure out that I was going the wrong way on a one-way street. Something even a language barrier will help you figure out when the locals are laughing and flailing their arms and pointing to, of course, a one-way street sign above their head!

After I turned myself around and quit giggling, I found myself in the neighborhood section not far from the airport. The pictures below are what I saw. One thing I learned is that the locals are only allowed to use their water during certain parts of the day. Everywhere I looked bright-colored laundry was hung out to dry in the warm sunshine.

No doubt, driving around for many blocks, poverty was living among them like a dirty, unwelcome rat. Within moments I found the main road near the ocean where the tourism and shopping began. There were literally 15-20 jewelry stores filled with gold and silver along a quarter mile stretch of beach-front property. Much activity filled the street as huge cruise ships were unloading hundreds of people anxious to find a bargain in Cozumel. Just a few miles down the road were where some of the beautiful all-inclusive resorts began…with, of course, an unlimited water supply and huge swimming pools.

What struck me that first day was the fact that as I drove through the poverty-hit areas a few blocks away from downtown,

I found nothing but smiling, happy people. Children on old bicycles laughing and playing, clunky old scooters zipping here and there carrying 2-3 people, at times, on one scooter. They were just happy all the while basking in this beautiful city! It certainly seemed to me they didn't know they were doing without. Maybe they had made peace with it all and choose to shield themselves from the glitz and glamour of their city knowing that's just not reality for them.

Everyone I met was very kind with big brown eyes, willing to help me even if I was lost, couldn't speak their language, and didn't know which direction to go! It amazes me still that in Cozumel paradise and poverty live so closely within reach of each other and life just.... well.... goes on. How true that seems of our lives many times. We are able and have the God-given right to be living in the neighborhood of 'paradise', but we choose to live on the streets of poverty within our minds and hearts. Living on Victim Street with no roadmap to escape. Deuteronomy 30:15 says "See, I set before you today life and prosperity, death and destruction. For I command you today to love the LORD your God, to walk in obedience to him, and to keep his commands, decrees and laws; then you will live and increase, and the LORD your God will bless you in the land you are entering to possess."

We are given such a promise and have the right to choose life...and a GOOD life! How MANY times I personally have chosen the wrong path, ignored the road signs pointing the right way and continued following into a place I should never have been in the first place! If you are in the midst of a wrong direction in your life....and you KNOW that you are headed down the wrong path...STOP and redirect your heart towards prosperity in your life and not death or destruction.

I am flailing my arms at you to say.... the Lord's promises are M-A-N-Y, and they are everlasting and stamped with a promise of his love and care for you. You absolutely matter! Today get a glimpse of your life in a state of 'paradise' which includes joy, health, love, peace, contentment, provision for more than enough and a FANTASTIC FUTURE beyond your wildest imagination! This is all within your reach but.... YOU MUST CHOOSE IT! Today, leave the streets of poverty including spiritual bankruptcy, stress, depression, discouragement, greed, or rebellion far behind you. Now you can walk into a much brighter future, and a life of paradise all your very own.

MARLENA COMPSTON

♥ Have riches owned you? Choose today to repent and ask God to place you on the right path of honoring Him in everything you do. Riches will NEVER satisfy us.

_____

_____

_____

_____

_____

Arms of Love

We can find great peace knowing in Psalm 18:30-36 that God is our refuge...He is our Rock, the One that arms us with strength...

As for God, his way is perfect:
The LORD's word is flawless;
he shields all who take refuge in him.
For who is God besides the LORD?
And who is the Rock except our God?
It is God who arms me with strength
and keeps my way secure.
He makes my feet like the feet of a deer;
he causes me to stand on the heights.
He trains my hands for battle;
my arms can bend a bow of bronze.
You make your saving help my shield,
and your right hand sustains me;
your help has made me great.
You provide a broad path for my feet,
so that my ankles do not give way.

Father, remind us that you are there ready to hold us up even when we feel we cannot possibly stand on our own strength. Ephesians 6 says to be strong in You and in the power of Your might. We may not be able...but You are WELL able. We may not feel strong but You, Lord God, are STRONG.

♥ We are at the end of The Hammock. How has this book helped your spiritual life? List moments that have drawn you closer to Him.

_____

_____

_____

_____

_____

_____

_____

_____

_____

_____

_____

_____

_____

_____

_____

_____

_____

In Closing

"May you walk gently through the world and know its
beauty all the days of your life."
Apache Blessing

My prayer for you is to know Him and continually seek Him.
My prayer is that you are healed and whole.
I would love to hear from you!
Marlenacompston@gmail.com

THE HAMMOCK
MARLENA COMPSTON